Countess of Chester Hospital

Postnatal Depression

Because your family matters ...

Family matters is a brand new series from Wiley highlighting topics that are important to the everyday lives of family members. Each book tackles a common problem or difficult situation, such as teenage troubles, new babies or problems in relationships, and provides easily understood advice from authoritative professionals. The *Family Matters* series is designed to provide expert advice to ordinary people struggling with everyday problems and bridges the gap between the professional and client. Each book also offers invaluable help to practitioners as extensions to the advice they can give in sessions, and helps trainees to understand the issues clients face.

Titles in the series:

Postnatal Depression

Facing the Paradox of Loss, Happiness
and Motherhood

Dr Paula Nicolson

University of Sheffield

JOHN WILEY & SONS, LTD

Chichester · New York · Weinheim · Brisbane · Singapore · Toronto

Other Wiley Editorial Offices

John Wiley & Sons, Inc., 605 Third Avenue,
New York, NY 10158-0012, USA

WILEY-VCH GmbH, Pappelallee 3,
D-69469 Weinheim, Germany

John Wiley & Sons Australia, Ltd, 33 Park Road, Milton,
Queensland 4064, Australia

John Wiley & Sons (Asia) Pte Ltd, 2 Clementi Loop #02-01,
Jin Xing Distripark, Singapore 129809

John Wiley & Sons (Canada) Ltd, 22 Worcester Road,
Rexdale, Ontario M9W 1L1, Canada

British Library Cataloguing in Publication Data
A catalogue record for this book is available from the British Library

ISBN 0-471-48527-6

Project management by Originator, Gt Yarmouth, Norfolk (typeset in 11.5/13 Imprint)
Printed and bound in Great Britain by Biddles Ltd, Guildford and King's Lynn
This book is printed on acid-free paper responsibly manufactured from sustainable
forestry, in which at least two trees are planted for each one used for paper production.

Contents

Contents

About the author

Dr Paula Nicolson is a psychologist who has been
researching in the area of women's reproductive health
and postnatal depression for over 20 years. She is currently Reader in Health Psychology at the University of
Sheffield School for Health and Related Research. She is
soon to become a grandmother.

In memory of Barbara Gullick

Foreword

My GP friend was expecting her first baby. She and I were part of a small group who were setting up a company. My friend said, 'When I finish work before the baby's born I'll take over the company's correspondence. I'm busy now but once the baby's born I'll have plenty of time.'

I said, 'No you won't. You won't have any time and your brain will have turned to mush.'

She ignored me. Time passed, her daughter was born, and the usual sleep and feeding problems followed. My friend was besotted with her baby. One day, when we were trying to discuss some business matters, she said to me, 'My brain has turned to mush.'

My friend has always been a competent, self-confident though modest person. On the scale of difficult babies hers is at the easy end. My friend has a very supportive husband, parents and parents-in-law. Yet, even she has found it impossible to maintain her usual level of self-confident, clear thinking. How much more difficult it must be for women who come to childbirth with serious doubts about their worth and competence, and who are not well supported by family and friends.

When we feel self-confident and competent, we are aware that there are a number of matters competing for our attention. We can put these matters in order of priority and focus appropriately on each as the need arises. Thus, we can deal with 'What shall I wear today?' quickly and move on to planning our day's work. When, in motherhood, our brain turns to mush, many matters which might need our attention disappear from the world we are inhabiting, and our focus is absorbed completely by a scrap of humanity who is now our one huge responsibility.

Moreover, when we feel self-confident and competent we can keep from our consciousness all those troubling thoughts, emotions and memories which, if we dwell on them, will undermine our self-confidence and sense of self-worth. But, once our brain turns to mush, these troubling thoughts, emotions and memories can break into our consciousness and attach themselves to our concerns about our baby and our ability as a mother. If you've been lucky enough to have had truly loving and supportive parents, if as a baby and child you had mostly good experiences of mothering (no mother is perfect: if she were her baby would have no reason ever to learn to look after himself) and if you're surrounded by people who constantly show you that you are loved and valued, troubling memories and feelings are not likely to be any more than a momentary problem. But, parents who did not love you, or if you've grown up telling yourself that your parents did love you while secretly fearing that they did not, if your own experiences of being bothered were not pleasant, if in childhood adults treated you badly and if now you are surrounded by selfish people concerned only with their own welfare, then, when your brain turns to mush, you can find it extremely difficult to keep at bay that host of horrible memories with their train of miserable, self-condemning thoughts and feelings.

It is self-condemnation which turns misery and sadness into the prison of depression. If you have learned, as many woman have, how to be an expert in feeling guilty and blaming yourself for whatever disaster might occur, you can, at any time in your life, turn the sadness which naturally follows loss and disaster into depression. For all women, motherhood involves the loss of freedom, the loss of irresponsible youth and the loss of the belief that you are always in control of your life and your body. For each individual woman, other losses can occur, while any woman who demands perfection in everything she sets out to achieve will find being the perfect mother a goal utterly beyond her reach.

For the expert in feeling guilty, self-blame comes into operation far more quickly than conscious thought can ever operate, and so depression can seem to appear out of the blue without any apparent reason. However, if we understand ourselves, if we recognise our well-practised skill in blaming and condemning ourselves, if we are aware how certain trains of thought, particularly about certain past events, can lead us into misery, then we can listen to the way we talk to ourselves and learn how to control and change our pernicious self-talk. Never again will we tell ourselves that we are useless, wicked and worthless. If, at the same time, we recognise how our nearest and dearest can hurt and belittle us, we can learn not to accept their bad feelings as our just punishment. Then we can devise strategies to protect ourselves against that hurt. There is no law that says you have to telephone your mother every day or that you must not confront your partner with his selfishness.

These are matters which are best dealt with before your baby is born. One of the many myths about postnatal depression used to be that pregnant women should not be told about the existence of PND, because then they would worry about it. This myth prevailed when the medical profession believed that PND could be explained solely in terms of changes in hormone levels. (There is no difficulty or disaster in a woman's life which a male doctor cannot blame on the state of the woman's hormones.) Now it is recognised that hormonal changes alone cannot explain why one woman becomes depressed after childbirth and another does not. What is now recognised as being extremely important is how the woman sees herself and what kind of support she gets from professional staff, family and friends. A woman cannot do anything about her hormonal changes, but there is much she can do in checking and perhaps changing how she sees herself and what kind of support she is being given.

What has been greatly needed by pregnant women, by the professionals who look after them and by the woman's husband or partner and her family and friends is a book written simply and clearly setting out what needs to be done if the woman is to meet the huge challenges of motherhood without her blaming herself for her failures and thus falling into depression. This is such a book. Paula Nicolson has combined a highly readable account of the concepts and research now forming the leading edge of the study of PND with reports of her sensitive and revealing interviews with women trying, and sometimes failing, to cope with the impact of motherhood on their lives. Other people's stories tell us much more than any recounting of facts, however skilfully that might be done. Out of these accounts and out of the practical advice which is found throughout the book, and added to at the end, every woman can give herself an excellent chance of experiencing fully the joys of motherhood.

This book should be read by every person, of whatever profession, who is involved in the care of mothers and babies, by men who can be shocked by the discovery that becoming a father involves more than one small sexual act, by older women who had their babies at a time when new mothers were not listened to but merely told what to do, and by every woman who wants to understand the marvellous and extraordinary process of becoming and being a mother.

Dorothy Rowe

Acknowledgements

I want to thank all the women who took part in the study and told me their own stories of pregnancy, childbirth and postnatal depression. I am also grateful to Dr Vivien Ward, who gave me the opportunity to write this book, to Sheila Kitzinger for her supportive and constructive comments and to my family and friends who ensured I had the time and support to finish it.

Introduction

Who should read this book and why

This book is about women's experience of the first year after childbirth and the feelings and changes in emotion and relationships that motherhood provokes. Researchers have shown that between one and two out of every ten women becomes seriously depressed during this period of their lives. This is only a small part of the picture. As many as 90% of new mothers experience *some degree* of weepiness and anxiety, especially during the first few days after delivery and most women become depressed, disheartened or feel low for short but significant periods of time *at least once* during that first year of motherhood. This is not only true of first-time mothers. Depression can occur *every* time someone has a baby or after some pregnancies and not others. Some women, for example those who are socially isolated, have very low incomes and poor housing, or who have a history of emotional illness, are more at risk than others. Even so – *depression after childbirth can affect anyone.*

Depression during that first postnatal year is usually referred to as postnatal or postpartum depression. This is *not* the same as the psychiatric condition postpartum or puerperal psychosis that affects a small minority of women who literally 'lose their minds'. The mass media have made much of this illness and referred to it as PND. I have no desire to deny the extent and intensity of the distress that this state causes to all concerned. But it only happens to 1 or 2 women in every 1,000. Experts continue to debate whether puerperal psychosis is a separate mental illness or just the extreme end of PND. They still do not know for certain.

Health-care experts generally define PND as *a depression that occurs during the first 12 months following childbirth.* Some say that it is 'atypical' – that is, that it is *dissimilar* from any other kind of depression that the individual woman would have experienced before. Other experts disagree. They see PND as distinct from other types of depression only in so far as it is associated with the aftermath of childbirth and the life events and changes brought about through motherhood. Recently, psychologists have argued that many women experience depression in the last stages of pregnancy and what is identified as PND might actually be *pre-natal depression* caused by bodily changes and psychological reactions to being pregnant. Theories about the *causes* of PND vary, from those who argue that PND is an illness caused by hormonal disruptions which take place during childbirth and early lactation to those who suggest that it is the social conditions of motherhood itself that are depressing to women. The majority believe that, probably, PND has several causes and that the life history and social circumstances of each woman give clues as to the origins of their distress.

What most women want to know is 'will it affect me?' and if it does 'what should I do?' It is these issues that are highlighted in this book. It answers some important general questions. Why are some women depressed in early motherhood and others not? What causes PND? Is it easily diagnosed or cured? Is it the result of hormonal or other biological problems? Is it 'madness' or is it simply the result of women 'wanting it all'? Are there any other explanations as to why as many as nine out of ten new mothers find themselves in tears and feel 'down' shortly after they have their babies, and at least one out of ten find themselves seriously depressed at some time during the first year of motherhood?

More particularly, the book takes a first-hand look at mothers' experiences of stress, anxiety and depression and answers their questions 'Why me?', 'Why do I feel this way?', 'How can I feel better?'

The book is based upon the stories of 24 women who talked to me while they were pregnant and several times during the first year after the birth of their babies. They came from all walks of life. They all lived in and around London in the UK, although some lived in the inner city and others in suburbs. Some of the women had full-time careers, some gave up work to become full time mothers. Several worked part-time to fit in with childcare arrangements. All had a relationship with the father of their baby, but not all were married to him or stayed married over the course of our meetings. Not everyone I talked to could be described as having PND. However, everyone had had some periods of feeling down, irritable, confused and anxious and some were very distressed at times. Their feelings and emotional reactions to their situations were for different reasons in every case and their expressions of distress took more than one form. What they had in common was that they were trying to negotiate their lives as mothers. They talked to me about the difficulties they faced with their self-esteem, relationships, self-confidence, work, practical aspects of their lives and the changes that becoming a mother can bring to all of these parts of our lives.

It is not only first-time mothers who face these kinds of problem. Some women manage their way through the tiredness, physical strain and change of lifestyle with only passing irritability and the occasional uncharitable thought. However, a woman who had sailed through a previous experience of new motherhood, might find herself seriously depressed after the birth of a subsequent child. And vice versa. It is the apparent lack of logic surrounding PND that taxes the mind of health professionals and researchers as well as those who are suffering.

Here I show how women can understand more fully the realities of motherhood from the psychological to the biological. What can women expect from their bodies, health-care services, their friends, partners and other family members?

Most importantly though, from my perspective as a psychologist, I illustrate the many available ways of gaining a clearer sense of self-knowledge to help cope with depression after childbirth, and how this links into other aspects of emotional life. Understanding PND and learning about feelings which emerge at this stage can also enable insight and a broader *self-awareness*. For example, one of the most difficult things for many women is recognising what *they themselves want*. New motherhood is a time when we learn how to care for another – someone who could not survive alone. This is a great responsibility. Sometimes, this is combined with increased domestic duties, which involve, again, doing things for others. Losing sight of your own needs is easy. Developing *your* sense of self-worth and making (reasonable) demands that reflect your needs is difficult.

A great deal has been written and talked about PND over the past 10 years; much of which has indicated that, somehow, depressed *women* are suffering from 'raging female hormones' or are mentally unfit. They chose motherhood and then cannot cope. They became mothers and then complained. If they remain depressed, their children may suffer intellectually and emotionally through lack of attention and stimulation. Their relationships suffer because it is very difficult to live with or have a close friendship with a depressed person, particularly if they appear to have everything they want and are still unhappy. Sympathy for a bereaved, divorced, sick person or accident victim is typically far greater than for someone with PND. But having PND is particularly distressing if combined with fear, guilt and self-blame. 'I wanted this baby and I should be able to cope.'

Having a baby and being a 'good' mother is taken for granted by most people as being the central part of being a woman. Despite the range of lifestyle choices available to contemporary women, many become parents. This is not necessarily because women *all* want babies without question. It is quite normal to be fearful about risks of infertility, pregnancy, giving birth and taking care of babies and children. We also know more now than in previous generations about the potential instability of marriage, difficulties surrounding child-rearing from infancy to adolescence and the opportunities for those women who remain childless. Motherhood is a serious challenge, but one which the majority of women still embrace.

Many women today, though, experience motherhood outside the traditional marriage, sometimes but not always as a matter of choice. It is generally acceptable to be a single mother, mother within a lesbian relationship, cohabit with the baby's father or live in a 're-constituted' family with a partner who is not the

father of your children. Contemporary women also expect
to play some part in life outside the home in paid employment. Again, patterns vary and some women only work
once the children are in school, while others maintain
careers following only brief maternity leave. Fewer
women, though, than ever before remain in the traditional
housewife/mother role.

What happens to you when faced with motherhood for
the first time? Few women experience the kind of concep-
tion, pregnancy and birth they expected. Few 'bond'
immediately with their baby, and that can be a
major setback. Individual physiological, psychological,
emotional, economic and social circumstances vary enormously, and all of these things influence the way women
mother children. Health professionals frequently advise
would-be mothers that they are unlikely to conceive the
first few occasions they try. However, many women do so.
Many women never conceive, or take years before they
become pregnant. Some conceive with ease the first time
and never manage it again. There is no consistent route to
motherhood.

Similarly, there is no uniformity about postnatal
experience. After labour, many find it difficult to care
about the infant that has been the cause of this pain and
exhaustion. Of the women I talked to, most wanted to
avoid that immediate post-birth time alone with the
baby – they wanted to scream out 'take it away, please!'
Others felt tears of joy and tenderness towards the infant.
Feelings about the very new baby ranged from intense
hatred, through ambivalence, awe and anxiety about its
well-being. In the majority of cases, warmth and affection
emerged before too long. These first encounters, though,
may have far-reaching consequences. Samantha told me
how distressed she had been for several weeks after a
difficult delivery. Forceps were used to ease the baby
into the world. But when she found herself faced with

this 'distorted', ugly red thing that was supposed to be her baby, she 'freaked'. The guilt of those early feelings towards her baby remained with her for several months.

Many new mothers are confronted by a further and more enduring paradox: the new baby is exciting and much wanted. But daily life can be devastating. It might feel to the mother that she has lost everything she once had and expected for the future. But there is no going back. You cannot return the baby. Motherhood, with its dilemmas and stresses, is not any indication of feeling for the baby. It is common to love the baby, but hate the things you have to do for it and the domestic 'captivity' that motherhood frequently imposes.

Postnatal depression, which is the label given to these feelings, comes in several forms and hits you hard. It comes when you least expect it and are least equipped to cope. You have had a baby, you are tired, anxious about your new skills and worried about the time you no longer have for your partner, your friends or yourself. Many women feel this way, as shown through the stories of those I interviewed.

Felicity was preparing for Christmas four weeks before her first baby's expected arrival. All of a sudden, as she was making the beds, she went into labour and within two hours 'I was lying there with this stranger between my legs – I had no idea what to do'. Her mind was still focused on preparations for her parents' Christmas visit to launch her maternity leave from work as a government scientist. 'Everything was upside down – I panicked. I had no idea how to cope.' She thought she would never get her life back to normal again.

Wendy's baby was born on time and according to plan. She and her partner were delighted. However, neither had imagined how much new parenthood would interfere with the renovation of their large Victorian house. They had both seen Wendy's maternity leave as a chance for rapid progression with the decorating! Both Wendy and Dave had a series of emotional crises, which ended when Wendy returned to work after three months. She felt better able to cope with her life, but by then both she and Dave had had to re-assess their relationship. Wendy felt she had grown up fast, while he had run away from the demands of parenthood.

Angela was particularly proud of the way she had coped with labour during the birth of her second baby. Eighteen months before that, she had cried with the pain, screamed at the midwives and been scared of what was happening to her body and the baby. This time, she had been in control. What neither she nor Mark, her husband, had anticipated, though, was how much work, money, time and energy were involved with caring for two babies. They coped with their lives showing stoical resilience. However, it was when Angela realised that she had not had time to take a bath for two days that she found she could not stop crying.

Felicity, Wendy and Angela, three intelligent, capable but separate women, each from very different social backgrounds, had each been shocked at the extent to which they *lost control* of their lives following the arrival of the new baby. All three faced crises of confidence and all three coped with them differently, and, as the months passed, each of their lives took different directions. These women each had a case of 'the baby blues' – weepiness, anxiety and feeling down – an experience shared by around 80% to 90% of all women having babies in contemporary Western societies.

A combination of sudden hormonal changes, the shock and pain of labour, the addition of the new baby into your life and the disruption this brings to your existing relationships, ideas, plans and expectations all conspire to make you feel that things around you are out of your control. We need to feel in control in order to cope with

the demands of family and working life. We need to feel
some degree of control over our physical health, body
shape, eating habits, sleep, finances and social life to
maintain a sense of well-being. Babies almost always put
a (temporary) stop to that. Parents think they can anticipate what those early days will be like – and are usually
wrong!

As time passes and everyone else's life returns to
normal, things may get worse for some women. You
may have had a longer night's sleep, but if you should
have a bad night, there are fewer volunteers to take over
the routine chores so you can catch up on it. You may now
have time to meet up with your friends, but find they are
doing things that are either so exciting that you feel a total
dullard, or they seem trivial and unappreciative of the
importance of the role you are now playing. You find
yourself withdrawing, not knowing where time has gone
or what you have done with it. The baby seems more
demanding and more difficult to occupy. You never
have enough time to shop, clean, care for the baby and
cook the evening meal. Your partner and friends seem to
be constantly critical of you (and you of them – but
silently). When you look in the mirror you see someone
you hardly recognise and there seems to be nothing you or
anyone else can do to change this state of affairs.

In what follows, the stories of the women I talked to
will be told to describe how childbirth and early motherhood can affect all of our lives. The book will focus on the
way feelings develop and change with time and adjust-
ments to social circumstances and emotional relationships. The paradox of new motherhood is that happiness
and loss co-exist. Satisfaction and pleasure compete
with frustration and distress for our state of mind.
Psychological survival requires a difficult juggling act
between the needs of your baby, your partner, your
family – and of great importance – yourself.

Being depressed

What is depression? – official and unofficial definitions

> *depression affects not only how we feel, but how we think about things, our energy levels, our concentration, our sleep, even our interest in sex. So depression has an effect on many aspects of our lives*[1].

> *you think you'll never pick up and you feel so very ill all the time and you get no relief from it whatsoever ... nothing is worth doing and you get no pleasure from anything at all*[2].

Depression is a paradox. It is the essence of hopelessness and despair. It has the potential to ruin your life and destroy relationships at home and at work. But it may also be the turning point – the opportunity for re-birth and personal development, if you manage to weather the storm and re-discover your strength. Depression is the typical response to a *loss* and bereavement. It is also common for depression to accompany dramatic life changes that on the surface represent the opposite of a loss – lottery wins, pregnancy, promotion at work, marriage or having a new baby.

Experts have different explanations about the *causes and effects* of depression. The most frequently rehearsed perspective on depression is the emphasis upon depression as an *illness*. Such a model is popular because it removes the stigma that sometimes accompanies psychological problems by showing that the depression is not the *fault* of the individual who is suffering. They have something *physically* wrong with them. They are not to blame as they have an illness that can be 'cured'.

This view, known as the *medical model*, suggests that depression is caused by an abnormality of brain behaviour. The brain either fails to produce or produces too much of the chemicals that control emotion and mood. Once the brain has lowered a person's mood, the body will follow.

Psychological models of depression are more complicated. Many contemporary psychologists advocate a *biopsychosocial model of depression* (Figure 1). That means that depression occurs as a result of previous mental distress, combined with specific 'risk factors' related to current circumstances such as social isolation and a particular 'trigger', or events such as a death in the family. Psychologists generally agree that the symptoms and experiences of depression have common features. However, they also acknowledge a complicated interconnection between *biological patterns* (brain behaviour or even some genetic predisposition), *psychological issues* (these can vary according to the characteristics of the unconscious mind, to styles of thinking or personality or a history of emotional distress of psychiatric disorder) and

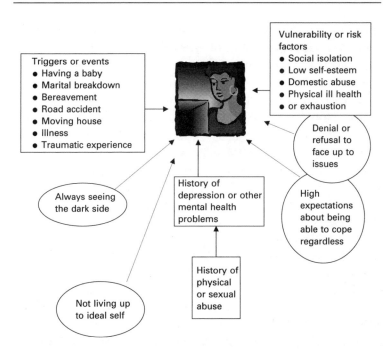

Figure 1 Bio-psychosocial explanations of depression.

the impact of the social context (for example, stress at work, domestic abuse or a bereavement).

Some writers see transparent and fundamental links between intimate relationships (or 'attachments'), loss of those attachments and psychological and emotional change. For instance, a child who loses a parent to death or divorce will suffer an extreme form of loss. An adult losing a partner, friend or even a much-regarded job may find it difficult to face the changes which are demanded of them as the inevitable consequences of the loss. Such experiences may be the triggers for psychological decline, which lead to clinical or even psychotic depression[3]. Alternatively, the changes following such a loss may demonstrate personal growth and the development of new-found confidence and strength. Through our experience of early attachments (usually to the parent or significant adult in charge of infant care), we see the relationship of our self to others in the world. We also begin to make sense of our inner, emotional lives in this way. Thus, a child whose parent is mostly available, caring, kind and supportive will not only want to maintain a wider world experience in which people behave in this way, but will also *see itself* as being worthy, valuable and essentially 'good enough'. They deserve their place in the world. So, if a person from a stable and supportive background suffers a deep and unexpected loss of a loved one, they will go through a grief reaction, but, at the same time, they will also be working consciously and unconsciously to achieve a resolution – to get beyond the grief and put it behind them. However, because they have lost a good and close relationship, they know they will not be the same and that the experience will change them. However, they will gain more self-knowledge and their demonstrated ability to get beyond their trauma will ensure them of the confidence that the pain will pass.

This explanation of the experience of depression describes a psychological process in which we *think* about the world and give it *meaning*. It is also about the way the unconscious mind operates to colour perceptions and experiences of the world. These issues will be explored in the context of the lives of the women who talked to me about their depression.

For many people, depression and deep unhappiness have their roots in emotional experiences that need exploration and psychological 'work' in order to overcome them. Drugs without self-understanding are not helpful in the long term, although for some women they may seem to be the only answer at the time.

What it feels like to be depressed

Clinicians frequently use the criteria laid down in the *Diagnostic and Statistical Manual of Mental Disorders* produced by the American Psychiatric Association, when diagnosing clinical depression in a patient. This manual provides a list of symptoms of which five or more need to be noted on most days and which represent a change from the way the person normally feels and/or behaves. These include:

- depressed mood (feeling sad or empty);
- diminished interest in pleasure;
- significant weight loss or gain, insomnia of hyper-somnia (too much sleep);
- agitation or the opposite – being slowed down;
- fatigue or loss of energy;
- feelings of worthlessness or excessive or inappropriate guilt;
- diminished ability to think or concentrate;
- indecisiveness and recurrent thoughts of death;
- thoughts of suicide or attempt at suicide.

The diagnosis of clinical depression is only valid if there is no other explanation of these symptoms (such as drug abuse or bereavement) and if the symptoms persist for more than two months.

There is much debate as to how convincing the diagnosis of an endogenous depression[4] of this kind might be. Janet Stoppard,[5] who has conducted research on women and depression for several years shows that the traditional clinical definitions of depression are not as 'objective' or 'scientific' as they are made out to be by clinical practitioners. She draws attention to the crucial importance of how the depressed individual reports and constructs the symptoms she describes to the health professional, who then provides a diagnosis. In other words, the gap between the feeling of depression and the self-assessment of the individual and the standard views and skills of the mental-health professional provides many opportunities for divergence.

Paul Gilbert, another psychologist, who has been treating depressed people and carrying out research in this area for years, also emphasises that, although we can describe depression reasonably accurately, *that does not mean that everyone's experience is the same.*

Who gets it and what causes it

Depression has been described and explained over the centuries and across most cultures in a variety of ways. Depression is the substance of literature and drama. It is romanticised through some heroes and villains. Heathcliffe, Mr Rochester and Hamlet – dark, brooding and powerful. It is only through personal accounts of depression that we can gain a sense of what depression *feels* like, and it is because these accounts are widely recognised that it is possible to say that depressed people share many experiences. Paul Gilbert describes his own experience of depression thus:

> *Depression is a horrible state to be in. Having worked with depressed people for many years and having heard many different stories, the thing that stands out is the sheer misery of it. Another way I encoun-*

tered depression was personally, nearly twenty years ago. In the context of some major setbacks in my life, I suddenly found myself caught up in one. Even though I had studied depression, I was not as prepared as I thought I would have been to deal with it. My depression was the milder kind but even so it was associated with panic attacks, many sleepless nights, a terrible sense of having failed in important areas of my life and a deep dread. Researchers rarely talk about dread, but I think it is a good word to sum up what people feel when they are depressed.

Martin Amis describes a man undergoing life-disturbing distress:

He awoke at six, as usual. He needed no alarm clock. He was comprehensively alarmed. Richard Tull felt tired, and not just underslept. Local tiredness was up there above him – the kind of tiredness that sleep might lighten; but there was something else up there over and above it. And beneath it. That greater tiredness was not so local. It was the tiredness of time lived, with its days and days. It was the tiredness of gravity – gravity which wants you down there at the centre of the earth. That greater tiredness was there to stay: and get heavier.[6]

Shakespeare also describes depression and how other non-depressed people see it well. Hamlet, filled with grief after his father's death and his mother's rapid re-marriage, was asked by the King '... why the clouds still hang on you?' and told by his mother to '... cast thy nighted colour off'. The images here are of clouds *hanging* – a shaded blackness and weighty matter that obscures his view of the world and the world's view of him. Hamlet responds to his mother's accusation that he is wearing his depression on his sleeve and overdoing his feelings of grief:

> 'Tis not alone my inky cloak, good mother,
> Nor customary suits of solemn black,
> Nor windy suspiration of forced breath,
> No, nor the fruitful river in the eye,
> Nor the dejected haviour of the visage,
> Together with all forms, moods, shapes of grief,
> That can denote me truly. These indeed seem,
> For they are actions that a man might play,
> But I have that within that passes show;
> These but the trappings and the suits of woe[7].

His behaviour, in crying and sighing, and appearance of total dejection and despair reflect the way he feels. It is often difficult for others to believe that a person might feel this way (at least for long). They think it is possible (and desirable) for the depressed person to snap out of it. Others feel somehow contaminated by the mood. Depressed people appear to have 'clouds' and 'blackness' surrounding them – they cast a gloom on others. They may be thought of as drawing attention to themselves in this way. But when you are depressed, this same blackness encompasses everything about you. It is inside, and what is *inside* you feels worse even than the blackness that onlookers perceive. And the world itself seems a worthless place. Hamlet goes on to say:

> How weary, stale, flat, and unprofitable
> Seems to me all the uses of this world![8]

Dorothy Rowe, an expert on depression and psychotherapist, makes a point of distinguishing between unhappiness and depression even though some of the symptoms are often held in common. She calls depression a 'peculiar isolation':

It is not simply loneliness, although in the prison of depression you are pitifully alone. It is an isolation which changes even your perception of your environment. Intellectually you know you are sharing a space with other people, that you are talking to them and they are hearing you. But their words come to you as if across a bottomless chasm, and even though you can reach out and touch another person, or that person touches you, nothing is transmitted in that touch[9].

Depression is often felt most acutely *exactly* when others try to reach out to you and you to them. The opportunity of contact, which you cannot return or respond to emotionally, leaves a greater gulf between the isolated individual and those who try to care. Depressed people do not simply languish in this state of isolation and despair, although others might think they do. Their minds and senses are most often inward-focused and their thoughts prevent them regaining their former selves. Depression is frequently combined with anxiety and panic – the fear that things are no longer the same and that nothing will ever improve adds to the vicious cycle.

Explaining depression

The 24 women whose experiences form the basis for this book volunteered to be part of the study which they knew

was to be about changes in mood following childbirth.
They also knew, when I met them during pregnancy,
that I would want them to describe to me what, if any,
experiences of depression they had had in the past and
how they had been affected by them. I wanted them to
tell their own stories of depression, but I was also aware of
the constraints that talking to someone with a tape recor-
der placed upon them. They were taking part in a research
study – they were not seeing me for therapy. This meant
that both the women being interviewed and I were
somehow 'outside' the emotions – we were co-researchers.
They were keeping an eye upon their emotional status for
me. They were not coming to tell me about their emotions
in order to get support or help. However, over time (both
the course of an interview and the year after the baby was
born) a relationship inevitably developed. Each one was
different, of course, and some may have seen me as the
'therapist' and others as the 'judge' of their mothering
skills. Traditional clinicians emphasise the objective
nature of clinical depression and describe it as somehow
distinct from the lives of the person who is depressed. This
is characteristic of the kind of contemporary psychiatry
and clinical psychology that uses the *medical model* as an
explanation for the causes and cure of a condition.
According to this approach, an individual becomes *ill*
and this illness needs an expert to diagnose, treat and
cure it. The cure is likely to consist of pharmacological
or surgical methods. There is sometimes an acknowledge-
ment that medical treatments are most likely to be effective when the 'patient' is relaxed and feels able to
understand the procedures that are being applied. But
this is a peripheral requirement.

The medical model is the opposite of the *holistic*
approach to health care in which diseases (which have
physical and/or mental manifestations) are seen and
treated as if they were integral to a person's life

experience – their history and current circumstances. Within this model, responsibility for identification of the roots of the problem and possible solutions are shared between the professional and the individual. I believe that holistic health care can include psychotherapy, although not all psychotherapists would see it this way.

Despite the cultural prevalence of the medical model in Western societies, most people who experience depression spontaneously provide an explanation. The explanation may be physical (rather than emotional or social); for example, 'I was depressed because I had had a serious illness which had left me physically drained'. Explanations sometimes involve comparison to others they know well or to the way they themselves had been in the past. But most people seem to want to *account* for the change from a non-depressed to depressed person in some way. Furthermore, as time passes, the explanations offered develop in their complexity. This does not appear to be an exclusively middle-class experience.

Samantha was brought up in a violent, unloving family in a tower-block flat which was eventually demolished and deemed unfit for habitation. Both her twin sister and mother made serious suicide attempts, and a brutal father placed the burden of caring for the family upon her. This does not appear to be the social context that enables self-awareness and reflection. However, she felt that, although she did have periods of feeling really down and depressed, somehow she understood that she could blame her parents for all the negative things that happened and not herself. In some ways, her twin sister's extremes of low mood helped Samantha identify and distinguish aspects of her own personality and life. She developed an ability to survive despite vulnerabilities, and recognised this strength in herself.

Gwen, who also contrasted her ability to cope, with that of her sister who was 'mixed up', explained her own episodes of depression as being out of the blue while also having a clear starting point – as a response to a particular event. She had had arguments with friends, she and her husband were short of money and they had taken in lodgers and she was also feeling very dissatisfied with her job at that time. 'The people were phoney and the work was boring – it was unbelievable. In the evenings I would sit and vegetate.' This made her put on weight, which had happened to her before in the past, and the thought of becoming increasingly fat made her panic. Also, her husband liked to be out playing rugby and spent more time at the club, even when there was no game. She joined him. 'They (the rugby club) were our social circle. But everything they said annoyed me. I felt I had to be nasty – and looking back and trying to analyse it – because I was so unhappy with my job and I thought I was too fat, too unattractive and too boring to talk to. Really not the person I really was.' Gwen went on to day that 'it sort of went on like that for about a year and then one day I decided that I was so unattractive to myself that I didn't want to be like that anymore.'

Although Samantha and Gwen's personalities and social backgrounds were very different from each other, both shared the desire to reflect on and place their bouts of depression in a context. That context enabled them to separate depression from their core sense of identities, and come to terms with the reasons and *value* the depression might have had in their lives. Both felt they learned from it. In Gwen's case, she believed she had learned that she needed to think carefully about her coping strategies when there was pressure on her. Samantha learned about her strength compared to others and also that, by reflecting upon how her personal strengths had helped her cope in the past, she could always see a way out of the depression.

We are not always strong enough to combat depression when it hits us. But most of us do learn from the experience, some even benefit and that is the key element of the paradox.

What is postnatal depression? Discovering the paradox

Different theories and different kinds of depression

PND presents two further paradoxes. Happiness and joy and the pride of being a mother may go hand in hand with depression, weeping and seeing the world as a pointless place. Becoming a mother has an impact on the life of the woman, each time it occurs, physically, socially, economically and emotionally. The ways in which motherhood affects each woman also crosses over into the lives of her baby, the baby's father, her family and friends. The success of the transition from pregnancy to motherhood has concerned experts and lay people alike. There are distinct rules, written and unwritten, that place the burden for the smooth transition and good mothering firmly upon the individual woman. When she fails to adapt to the role of mothering an infant, she is identified as having PND.

There is also a second paradox – which is illustrated by the level of attention that researchers and (some) clinicians place upon women's postnatal distress.

When I first began work on postnatal depression, I was keen to make the point that PND as such 'did not exist'. The notion of PND, as an illness, seemed to me to be making women and their physical capacity for giving birth and social demands, to take the primary-care role for the baby into people with deficiencies. That is, they were seen as, somehow, not being up to the job. Psychiatrists and obstetricians wanted to find out what was *wrong* with women. I wanted to explore the problems with the role of motherhood. Ann Oakley had been writing for some time, before I started my study, about the poor quality of the research and thinking about the conditions of birth and motherhood and the sloppy way that PND was defined. She identified clear differences between depressed moods, the transitory blues and clinical depression[1].

My proposal, based on research interviews, was that depression in the first postnatal year was a sensible response to the aftermath of birth and the pressures of motherhood in the contemporary social context, where women already have so many responsibilities and a new baby simply adds to them. I also argued that the contradictory ways in which motherhood equates with loss (of time, autonomy, social life, previous patterns of relationships, working roles and so on) indicates that PND may be, in part, a grief reaction.[2] At that time, PND was tautologically defined as being a depression that occurs in the first year after childbirth, and it was also seen as and illness and 'atypical'. My thesis testing this concept was challenged as naive.

Since that time though, researchers have shown that many women are depressed in middle and late pregnancy and that PND may be more closely related to that ongoing state than any postnatal one.[3] Also, definitions of the types

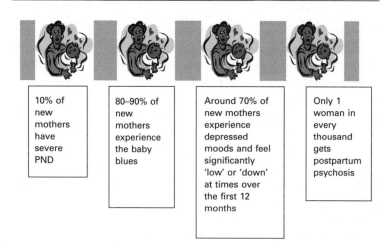

| 10% of new mothers have severe PND | 80–90% of new mothers experience the baby blues | Around 70% of new mothers experience depressed moods and feel significantly 'low' or 'down' at times over the first 12 months | Only 1 woman in every thousand gets postpartum psychosis |

Figure 2 The incidence of postnatal depression.

or categories of depression experienced during the first postnatal year have been honed down so much so that, now, PND (or postpartum depression as it is called in North America) is routinely defined as having symptoms equivalent to the American Psychiatric Association definition of clinical depression and starting within four weeks after delivery. This neatly disposes of the experience of the majority of women, more than one in every seven of whom get depressed moods, which may last for days and recur; women who identify themselves as feeling very 'low' or 'down' and have symptoms of anxiety and feel unable to cope. They frequently feel they have lost touch with who they really are and need social and emotional support, and even professional help, to get them through this time of great stress (Figure 2).

This, then, is a further paradox – depression at this stage is a normal and rational reaction to what is happening and shouldn't be defined as a clinical condition of PND. However, as researchers and clinicians shift that definition more towards those who are clinically

depressed or on the borderline of having a clinical
condition, the group of women who are suffering from
intermittent depression lose professional 'sympathy'.
They are thus in danger of becoming seen, and perhaps
more importantly seeing themselves, as people who
should pull themselves together. They are simply
whingers and moaners and should be grateful for what
they have!

The postnatal period, then, has become a site for lively
debate between researchers and health professionals from
different backgrounds. Medical, midwifery, nursing,
psychological, social and lay childbirth experts all
believe they can contribute to the mother and baby's
well-being at this stage. The focus of their attention is
about what has gone wrong for a woman if she should
become depressed. What causes PND? Who gets it? Can
it be predicted? What is its incidence? Will it happen more
than once to the same woman? These are questions which
have not been answered to the satisfaction of all who have
an interest in this area. What is clear, though, is that about
eight out of ten women experience some degree of depression and despair during the days and months after the
birth of their baby. As outlined in the Introduction, this
depression varies between the apparently transitory
experience of the 'baby blues' which experts attribute to
hormonal changes – depressed moods that last for days or
even a week or two over the course of the first year
following the birth – and clinical depression or a depressive disorder which is sustained depression over several
weeks and months which corresponds to the American
Psychiatric Association classification described on p. 15.

The women in this study were interviewed with this
model of the three types of depression in mind. I timed
the interviews so that they occurred just after the 'blues
stage' and, then, over the course of the year to identify the
length of time and type of depression that might be

experienced, and compared this with the circumstances surrounding the care of the baby at the time[4].

The baby blues

Katherina Dalton, a Harley Street gynaecologist, researcher and expert on PND, believes that depression after childbirth is the result of a hormone imbalance, which may be treated by giving the woman progesterone. She says that 'crying is the most characteristic symptom of the blues: [the mother is] sobbing when she should be smiling joyously.'[5] This demonstrates a limited understanding of how the paradox of depression works. 'Giving birth' is frequently talked about as if it just happens, and, when it is over, a new baby is there and the family has increased in size. Birth is not like that – it is painful, and labour can be unexpected and long. It can be frightening. Things may appear to go wrong, and they do sometimes go wrong. Intervention to put things right may be particularly frightening and stressful. The outcome is most often a healthy baby and mother who has come through the process relatively unscathed. Hormone fluctuations and deficiencies in the days after delivery may be the least of what is upsetting to the woman. Childbirth is an exciting event. Hormone fluctuations during the latter part of pregnancy are brought to a dramatic conclusion following birth and with the beginning of lactation. Also, labour is tiring, painful and potentially frightening as well as exciting. Childbirth often involves intervention, for example by Caesarean, an epidural to aid a forceps delivery or an episiotomy. All of these have physical and emotional consequences. It would be surprising, then, if such an experience did not have repercussions. However, the traditional research, which explores the relationship between PND and birth, makes the focus of study the physiology of the event rather than the physical and emotional context.

Hilary, giving birth to her second baby, was determined to have a normal delivery. She had been persuaded, against her better judgement, to have a Caesarean on the first occasion:

> *They decided they had to monitor the baby by putting something on her head. Then they said 'oh nothing's going to happen until morning' and I thought 'God I don't think I will be able to stand this'. I was so tired. I had terrible backache. I was rolling around in agony moaning to myself. About 8.30 a.m. he [the registrar] came back and said 'she's alright'. But another one came in about 9.45, and said 'you've got to push this baby out'.*
>
> *No one said at the time she was stuck (I saw it on the notes later). She then came out with a bang! Crash! But there wasn't a bruise on her head. I was very impressed but I was in a terrible state.*

Hilary had been terribly torn by the birth, and, although she didn't feel it particularly at the time, she had to have a great many stitches and it was months later before the pain in her perineum finally disappeared. Her muscles and back were also very painful and sore. She was particularly pleased with the way she had coped with the vaginal delivery and delighted with her baby, but her body felt seriously wrecked. The pain further reduced her ability to sleep, and being so badly wounded and having to care for a new baby and older child was almost unendurable for several weeks. Fortunately for her, her husband was supportive and took a share of the load. Hilary cried and was distressed in the first few days and weeks. But was this the blues and PND? Was it the result of progesterone deficiencies or the result of the physical punishment she had received on top of the new childcare responsibilities?

There are, sometimes, aspects of the birth experience which bring about immediate postnatal distress and weepiness which are the result of emotional and psychological as well as physical factors. Sarah, after her son was born, said:

> *One of my fears was that I wouldn't like him or take to him. I thought he was wonderful and I was on a high. Only an hour later – did I start crying! I was overcome with the tiredness and so many sensations. I just wanted to look at him and cuddle him – but my legs felt as if they were going to fall off. I was so wound up and my tension always goes to my legs. They just really ached. Also there were two other people who were brought down (to the postnatal ward) later. I got no sleep that night – in fact I got no sleep in the hospital for the full five nights.*

Those, like Dalton, who believe that the maternity 'blues' are physiological, transitory and self-limiting describe the experience as more of a joke and embarrassment to nursing and medical staff than a problem. Dalton says that other symptoms (apart from crying) of the blues are fatigue, poor concentration, slowness to learn new skills associated with the baby, confusion and anxiety about things to do with the baby and hostility to the husband. Identifying the blues, as Dalton does here, as (to quote a mother in her book) a 'fit of the fed-ups which goes before it comes', is to trivialise the experience. Taking responsibility for the physical care of a baby is potentially

traumatic, and some women will find it far more difficult
than others. It has long been argued that, although women
might have a burning desire to become mothers, the
'maternal instinct' does not extend to the automatic
ability to change a dirty nappy or prepare a bottle of
baby formula.

Several of the women in my study had had cause to
remember their experience of childbirth and their treatment on the labour and postnatal wards in a negative
light, which sometimes left scars. I shall talk more about
these and their potential effects in the next chapter.

Postnatal distress and depressed moods

It is sometimes difficult to distinguish between someone
who suffers from severely depressed moods and someone
with a borderline clinical disorder. Both are likely to have
those feelings of distance from others and from themselves, of hopelessness, powerlessness and despair.

However similar classic symptoms of depression may
be, depression, like everything else, appears in the specific
context of an individual life story. This means that each of
us responds in our own way to tackling the situation,
depending upon our previous experience, our personality
and the kind of people we have around to support us.

Suffering from depressed moods means that a great deal
of the time someone feels 'down' or 'low' for no immediately
apparent reason. This might be the result of what Vivienne
Wellburn[6] has called 'cabbage days'. She says that:

> The mother-at-home risks loneliness, boredom and
> feelings of fragmentation and demoralisation, [there
> can be a] feeling of being nothing, of losing yourself.

'Self-esteem is not possible if there is no sense of self.' This, Wellburn argues, can lead towards a more serious depression. These are days when time is spent on routine childcare and perhaps household tasks that are not particularly satisfying or stimulating. Feeling too tired or depressed to carry out those tasks, however, is likely to make everything seem worse, which, if not recognised, possibly leads to a spiral of depression.

Felicity, a government scientist three months into her first motherhood, was explaining the contrast between only having the baby and home to think about and having extra but more intellectually stimulating activities. She had been given one or two small pieces of work to do on the computer at home following a brief office meeting she attended. She explained how she had been at home thinking of the problems she still had feeding her premature baby:

> 'It was a mega-operation – it still is, but it becomes more normal when I have other things to do. I can now do it and not worry'.
> I got very tired (at home just looking after the baby). I can't quite remember what happened, but I was trying to do more and for a long time I didn't do much except look after him. I took him to a meeting at the office and I did some work which was quite good. I worked here, at home on the computer with him over one arm feeding!

She had been trying to find things around the home to occupy her, so she would not be bored and make the most of her maternity leave to catch up on those domestic things she would never otherwise have had time to do. For example, she had started doing some decorating. But that did not really work. These activities didn't stop her getting depressed, and the tasks didn't get done either because of the routine of looking after the baby and her role in charge of the household chores:

> *I was looking around the house yesterday and all around the house are unfinished jobs. Things I was going to go through at some point – washing up half finished. Because what happens is you get halfway through something and then you have to stop. I find I can't read the paper except the odd article.*
>
> *I can't concentrate and even if I could I don't have the time. And I am really tired. But I don't know why because he's started to go through the night. I don't know. I find that I watch television but I don't really see it ... I really don't know why I can't watch television. I think there's always a distraction. There are always other things to do. I don't have the interest.*

Felicity did not like to say she was depressed, but she certainly had many of the symptoms. Fatigue, poor concentration, anxiety about feeding the baby, a lost sense of time, little sense of enjoyment in anything and, at times, feeling overwhelmed by what she needed to do. However, for her, the brief glimpse of her returning self – that is, the competent scientist – was enough to shake the potential for a prolonged bout of depression. The uplift itself didn't last for long, but she realised that she was still able to be the person she previously valued as well as being the mother of a valued son. The glimpse of her former self also enabled her to face some of the feelings she had previously had about the baby. She said, 'I did not realise how much of an unresponsive lump a baby was.' However, as she realised that time at home was now short, she said that she was pleased he had been born in the winter so she could enjoy the summer with him. 'I now see he is getting more interesting and other people enjoy him more too.'

Not everyone is like Felicity with a dual interest in home and career.

Natasha, from a working-class background, had gratefully given up her office job in order to have her baby, but she did do some home hairdressing for financial reasons. She felt depressed because things had changed in her life in such a way that she could not envisage a return to the person she had been, and whom she had liked. She saw herself in the past as young, sociable, lively and physically attractive with a boyfriend who found her attractive and wanted to be with her. She had taken the next stage of the motherhood dream of marriage and living happily ever after to her heart, but was shocked to find the everyday contrast in her real life. Her partner worked later and later at night, claiming the need to earn overtime. She felt a strong tie to the baby and when she did manage to go out with her partner 'she's [the baby] on my mind all the time'. She also felt very differently about the time she spent with her friends:

> *Well, whereas before I'd probably be really 'mad' – I won't so much now. And what I wear. Like on Saturday I wanted to wear my leather mini-skirt – but I had second thoughts. I don't know why. Yeh – I'm a mother now, that sort of thing.*

She enjoyed her outing but 'very slightly differently – only slightly'. She put this down to awareness that she is a mother and that mothers are not 'outrageous' in ways she used to be and enjoy. Natasha also surprisingly (to her) missed going to work '... not so much the actual

work – but coming up to Christmas. I always remember
having such a great time!'

Thus the paradox – PND does not exist – but if
'cabbage days' go on too long and lead to depressed
moods, there is a risk of more prolonged and severe
depression. Depressed moods should not be trivialised
by the woman herself, health professionals or researchers.
However, for most women in Western industrial societies,
they comprise the lifestyle of the primary infant carer.

Postnatal depression

One woman in every ten is reported as having 'full blown'
PND. The symptoms have been described and discussed
above. But why does it happen and who is likely to get so
depressed? There are differing views as to how the categories of depression which women experience in the first
few weeks and months following childbirth link with each
other. For example, is a woman who experiences the blues
after the birth more likely to get severely depressed than
one who does not? Is someone who has depressed moods
more likely to experience clinical depression than
someone who has not had these mood changes? Is a
history of poor mental health going to lead to depression
after childbirth? Is having PND with one child going to
guarantee a recurrence with the next one? Ann Oakley
proposed long ago that:

> *Postnatal depression is not a 'scientific' term, but an
> ideological one. It mystifies the real social and
> medical factors that lead to mother's unhappiness.*[7]

Her plea was that women's reactions following childbirth should not be seen as deviant, but should be explored in their own terms and within the context in which the mothers were leading their lives. Women's experiences of postnatal unhappiness are not symptomatic of individual maladjustment or poor functioning (whether connected with psychological predisposition, hormones or lack of appropriate support networks). There are sensible reasons for women's postnatal distress and labelling it 'illness' does not help.

Katherina Dalton has long been an advocate of seeing PND as both atypical (that is, qualitatively different from depression experienced by non-mothers and by the mother at another time of her life) and caused directly by a hormone imbalance following pregnancy, birth and lactation. She also believes it can be cured by prescribing progesterone. Justification for PND as different from other types of depression is characterised by Dalton as follows:

> *The early mornings are usually the worst time of day for those with typical depression, and then they improve as the day goes on. By contrast, women with postnatal depression are often at their best in the morning, but the depression and inability to cope with the routine work comes on during the day. They feel worse in the evening and want to go to bed early.*
>
> *Typical depression is characterised by a loss of appetite with a revulsion from food, which in turn leads to a loss of weight ... in a matter of months. ... With postnatal depression the problem is different, the appetite is increased and the woman is always thirsty, continually tucking in to fattening foods and drinking mugs of tea or coffee to while away her hours of solitude. She may have odd*

cravings where she gorges on bars of chocolate, stacks of toast and honey, or piles of donuts or sticky buns.[8]

This seems a naive distinction between classical depression and atypical postnatal depression. First, there is a clear indication even in the *Diagnostic and Statistical Manual* that sleep patterns for depressed people vary. While it is frequently the case that (normally) depressed people awake early – the new mother is so unlikely to be in a situation where her sleep routine is normal, that it would be impossible to make any diagnostic assessment of her patterns of sleep and wakefulness. Second, the majority of depressed mothers carry on with their childcare tasks and are highly likely to become very tired by the evening because of the 24-hour, 7-day a week routine of infant care. Third, the eating patterns suggested by Dalton as symptoms of an atypical depression are more likely to be the search for a quick increase in blood sugar and energy levels. The increase in weight, which is likely to follow such eating habits, may in itself be depressing. Dalton's descriptions, in direct contrast to her philosophy, lend further support to the idea that there is no such thing as a distinct PND.

Through maintaining the illness model of PND, women's lives remain invisible. What happens to women at home with babies? What is it like to be a full-time mother and housewife rather than being in employment? What is it like to have contact with health-care professionals, who are experts on how you should care for and raise your child, telling you what to do? What is it like to have problems breastfeeding when you are alone at home with older children and a husband to care for?

Individual circumstances and the social conditions surrounding motherhood conspire potentially to make mothering a monumental burden, while the social myth persuades us all that motherhood results in happiness. Typical images of motherhood revolve around it being a major source of women's self expression and satisfaction; rarely do women picture themselves, in advance, as selflessly giving, ignoring their own needs and desires and experiencing loneliness and isolation. To subscribe to this dominant myth means that the early days and months of motherhood have a double impact. The inevitable stress, exhaustion and the burden of childcare are set against each woman's fear that she is somehow 'doing it wrong'. Her experience does not relate to her dream. It is no surprise then when some women and families 'buy in to' the ideology of PND. Esther Rantzen[9] publicly upheld the view that depression after childbirth is a clinical condition, declaring herself to be a victim and attempting to offer support to others so they should not feel any shame or take the blame for being unhappy. Other writers have argued that women suffered until PND was taken seriously. There is some important truth in this position, which will be discussed further in Chapter 3.

What causes postnatal depression? Why me? Why now?

Different approaches to understanding women's postnatal experiences

Having a baby is often a reason for happiness and celebration. Depression after childbirth causes emotional pain and suffering that lives side by side with the joy. That is the underlying paradox, and it is that paradox that frequently leads to a sense of bewilderment and guilt. Why do I feel so sad when I am so happy? I must be a bad mother.

Most women who have babies have PND to some extent, but some women's experiences are more extreme and prolonged than others'. Although it is the minority of new mothers who become *clinically* depressed, this condition still affects one in every ten women. These women represent a *significant proportion* of new mothers.

In Chapter 2, I outlined the ways in which health professionals and researchers disagreed about the *nature* of PND as well as the causes. It is likely that PND does not have a single *type* of cause. Although the character-istics of depression at this stage of a woman's life (tiredness, anxiety, feeling distressed and depressed and so on) are common features for everyone who suffers in this way, the impact and meaning of those feelings depends very much on each person's life history and what is happening to them at the time. The extent to which you are supported, the quality of your relationships with your partner and other children, financial circum-stances, educational level, employment prospects and previous emotional health all contribute to your post-natal state of mind. The immediate effect of the pregnancy, birth and postnatal care received from health professionals and feelings about the baby are also important.

I have outlined some of the issues identified as causing PND from hormonal fluctuations, stress in the delivery or postnatal wards, loss of a sense of autonomy and self-esteem, the 'cabbage' effect, personal history and the ways in which an individual copes with intermittent depressed moods. In this chapter, I look at the different experiences of the women I talked to – the background to their feelings of depression and their pathways to coping.

Trauma following birth

Childbirth is never easy – but some experiences are more predictable, manageable and less stressful than others. Ann Oakley[1] studied a group of new mothers from preg-nancy to a few weeks after the birth of their baby and found that a traumatic birth often led to depression. Extreme cases of stress during birth have been identified as leading to post-traumatic stress disorder (PTSD). PTSD is a clinical disorder or a syndrome.[2] Its symptoms are grouped into three types:

1 re-experiencing the traumatic event, through constantly re-enacting it in your mind and dreaming about it;

2 numbing or reduced involvement in the external world, as if you are at a distance from things that are happening to you;

3 a diverse group of symptoms such as memory impairment, difficulty in concentrating, hyper-alertness (being overaware of what is going on – 'jumpy').

Some people have a few of these symptoms all the time and others sometimes and other people have a clearly defined PTSD. That means they experience most of these symptoms all or most of the time. People who have these symptoms are also likely to feel worse when faced with a situation that reminds them of the trauma. So, if you have survived a train crash, you might be coping well and not thinking about the experience until you have to get on board a train or see a crash on television. That might make you break out in a sweat, tremble and have nightmares. This experience can last for a few hours or a few days. It might go away and then re-surface. Researchers Suzanne Lyons and Sarah Allen have demonstrated this.[3] Both researchers, in separate studies, have recorded the experiences of new mothers who experienced the birth as a form of torture and had extreme anxiety or flashbacks for months afterwards. It is difficult to predict who will have PTSD or related symptoms, even after a well-recognised traumatic event such as being involved in a car crash, a war, a fire or surviving a personal attack. There is an interaction between personality, emotional history and other life events around the time of the trauma itself. Like depression, what actually happens or the thoughts that depress you depend on personal history and current circumstances.

The women I interviewed included those who experienced the birth of their baby as a trauma, which stayed with them long after the baby was home and they had recovered physically. Jerri was living with her fiancé Tom, whom she had met a year beforehand through her work as a receptionist at a health club. She had had a difficult life. Her parents she described as cold and rejecting to both her and her younger brother. She had been a survivor, looking after her brother emotionally. When she left school and then home, she 'went off the rails' having a good social life which involved her in too much drinking. However, she would not have missed that time in her life, although she ended up hating that person she used to be. About a year and a half before I met her, her young brother had been killed in a car accident and this completely devastated her. The relationship with Tom (who was also younger than her) helped her a great deal, but such a blow is not easily overcome. Jerri had had an emergency Caesarean which she did not anticipate. But the worst thing about it for Jerri was the way that the health professionals handled it. She arrived at the maternity unit for what she believed was her final antenatal check-up. She was concerned at that time that her waters may have broken and (as is common, particularly with a first baby) she was two days past her predicted delivery date. During the course of that appointment, the midwife told her that while she had been incorrect in believing her waters had broken, she had started labour. She was admitted, and then discharged fairly soon after and told that it was a false alarm:

> *so I came home. It started again and I was in agony all weekend. But I didn't want to go back [to the hospital]. But the contractions weren't regular – so they said [on the phone] 'don't come in'. I didn't sleep all weekend and on Monday I had an appointment with the clinic. I had dilated by 4 centimetres and I was admitted. They were a bit short with me. I don't know whether they were trying to cover up – but they were short and said 'you should have been more persistent and come in'! They broke my waters at midday Monday. I hadn't slept for 3 days at that stage. I was using mind over matter to keep cheerful.*

The 'excruciating' pain then began. She was given various painkillers. She couldn't pass water so her urine was drained via a catheter.

The midwives were 'horrible' to her (she believed) because labour was progressing so slowly. When they said after several hours of trying that she was to have an emergency Caesarean by epidural, she thought 'I'm going to die now':

> *Tom said he wanted to be with me. But one of those horrible nurses said 'are you married?' He said 'no' and she said 'you can't come in then'. He insisted and the woman was overruled. I didn't feel anything then ... I was absolutely petrified. It didn't take long and I swore at him [the baby] and didn't feel very close to him at all.*

She cannot remember much that happened after that. I asked whether she had held the baby and she said she had, but only because it had been on her hospital notes.

She felt relieved and reasonably happy after a sleep but did not want to hold the baby. 'I was scared to be asked to see him.'

On the fifth day she was tearful, but the midwives told her that 'I was supposed to!' Then a nurse said she had to have an enema and Jerri (who normally did what she was told) refused:

> *I didn't want to be touched. I had this thing with my body. That made me cry because they thought I was being awkward. I was in tears and she said 'you've got to have one'. Apparently it was as if I had had a stomach operation and had got wind.*

After a while and more pressure from another nurse, they left her alone. Her fiancé had come into the maternity unit each time to feed the baby and change the nappies. Jerri didn't want to. Tom didn't find it odd (she thought) because he really enjoyed it, and so she believed that he didn't notice her rejection of the baby at that stage. However, a week after she returned home, her fiancé had to work. He would still come home at lunchtime. When he was away from her, though, she felt 'very lonely' and 'very scared'. She had several friends who wanted to come to see her but she only wanted Tom near her. This only lasted a few days and then she let her friends visit. Lack of sleep (even though Tom took turns at feeding through the night) made her nerves 'raw'. Her early feelings to reject the baby (which soon changed to love and a 'fascination') made her feel very guilty and ashamed, and she believed that this increased her anxiety about the baby's health. 'I thought I would be prepared for anything – but I find it difficult to cope with the mental worry of how they are – like if he's asleep you check his breathing.'

From the start she had anxiety dreams. She dreamed that the baby was drowning in a fish tank and that she could not move to rescue him. She constantly felt as if she needed to 'think deeply', which she said is 'not depression'. She would look at him, his perfection and think 'Oh what is the future for you?' She would worry:

> 'Is anything going to happen to you?' and that would make me cry. It's a very pessimistic way of thinking. Depressing. 'Oh here you are, but what's the point of life?' I did get very deep for a couple of days there, and, if I'd been prone to depression, that would have been the start of it. Because I really did wonder 'what's it all about?' I was thinking 'here you are and you are wonderful – but when are you going to die?' Then I snapped out of it as I do. I thought – forget about this and then I got over it.

She had long-term memories of the hostile behaviour of the midwives towards her and to her fiancé, and the argument which took place while she believed her life was in danger. She felt that, at the time of the birth, her body had been 'violated'. As a result, she felt numbed by this episode, and she continued to dream about it and have intrusive thoughts for months afterwards.

When Simon, her baby, was around 3 months old, she told me that she still lay in bed at night and thought about the birth, although she tended not to talk about it. Time passing had made her feel easier about the thought of her body being touched:

Jerri: *I think about the operation [Caesarean section] and I feel it's really horrible. I can't stop myself from thinking about it – it comes into my mind every now and then – what happened. Even the way I was treated in the labour ward was horrible. That goes through my mind a lot. I left my dignity on the doorstep when I went into hospital. [Laugh] Not that I had much to start with!*

Paula: *So it takes a long time to get over?*

Jerri: *Yes although I'm not so 'oh I don't want anyone touching me' any more that's gone. Probably as I've healed up a bit.*

At the time of the fourth interview (when Simon was over 6 months old), Jerri still thought that something terrible might happen to him. She also felt that about Tom her fiancé, which had only developed since the baby's arrival:

I worry about all aspects. I think of Tom 'Oh God what if he went out and didn't come back?' I say to him every time he goes out 'drive carefully please'. I don't say to him 'because I think you might die', but I secretly think that. It's constantly with me. I was surprised when I read this article which said it's a real sign of depression.

On every occasion I met with Jerri there was evidence that she had in the past or was currently experiencing some bouts of depression, but depression was something she herself only attributed to very extreme reactions – such as she had felt with the grief after the loss of her brother. Even then, though, she talked about snapping out of it – she considered that depression was something that you had a responsibility to control. This denial of her feelings and expectation of control possibly contributed to the depression and intrusive thoughts and dreams reminiscent of PTSD. Individual responses to trauma reflect the nature of the trauma, but there is also a complex relationship between that and the circumstances, emotional history and personality of the person involved.

Factors influencing PTSD?

There are three important factors that influenced Jerri's experiences in those early postnatal months:

1 The trauma of having to have *an emergency Caesarean* (the news of which made her think she was going to die) in a context that had already involved poor handling of the birth by successive health professionals, which made her feel very anxious and angry. The physical pain and its after-effects she associated with the dire treatment she received, thus she felt unwilling to be touched. The fear that Tom would be sent (and actually go) away intensified her fear. She also associated the baby's arrival with this 'torture', so swore at and then rejected him. She must have felt some guilt about her immediate feelings towards him, causing embarrassment and perhaps the fear that her lack of 'gratitude' would mean he might be taken away from her.

2 Jerri's *personal vulnerability* at the time of the birth. She was still grieving for her brother, and had gone through the experience of meeting and living with Tom and pregnancy in a relatively short period of time. This was welcome and positive, but even the most positive life events can be what psychologists call 'vulnerability factors'. She clearly associated her thoughts and feelings about her brother's death with Tom and feared for his safety, and this was compounded by thoughts about the baby's life and possible death as well.

3 *The legacy from cold, rejecting parents.* This led to a sense of self-blame, worthlessness and responsibility for everything that happens. When she told me of her brother's death, the first time we met, she said she had had a very strong feeling from her parents that they had wished it had been she who had died, not her brother.

It was none of these factors, alone, that brought about Jerri's response to the events surrounding the birth. If the hospital staff had been better trained and taken a mother-centred perspective, then they may have helped her through the stresses and fears which surrounded a difficult birth. If Jerri had become pregnant at a different stage of her life, then the trauma may not have taken root in her mind in the way that it did. The important point here is that, because she had good social support from Tom at first, when she felt so particularly rejecting of the baby and her friends, and then she had friends around her, she got over the experience.

Many women hide the distress that birth trauma can bring to their lives. Sheila Kitzinger, the childbirth expert has observes that women who have had a difficult time in labour are initially numb – relieved that the trauma is over. This state might last for weeks, months and even years. Then the floodgates can open, releasing complicated feelings and emotions, and a woman who has had an emergency Caesarean can be particularly vulnerable. Sheila Kitzinger is clear that these feelings of violation and distress are distinct from postnatal depression:

> *These women have their birth experience going round and round in their heads like a video on a loop. They can't switch it off. They are constantly reliving the trauma but rarely getting continuing support to deal with it. We need to find out what is most useful to women in this situation and what makes them feel worse. Then we can provide effective, individually-tailored support.*[4]

Worrying about the baby's health and welfare

Lynn, who was 31 when we first met, had been working in local politics and confident in herself professionally. She came from a loving and supportive family, and her parents and grandmother between them made themselves available to look after her and the baby for the first three postnatal months even though they didn't live in London.

Lynn was successfully and happily married and the couple planned to have their baby at home with a community midwife in attendance. They had an excellent relationship with the midwife, who was very experienced and supportive. Most of the labour took place as planned, but Lynn was surprised that after about 12 hours she felt she was losing control and suffering so much pain that a few hours later she went to hospital to have an epidural. 'In my NCT [National Childbirth Trust] Class when I was asked my worst fear – mine was ending up in hospital.' However, she was exhausted and couldn't cope any longer. Because she had deliberately paid no attention to any antenatal information about epidurals, she became increasingly frightened, but 'by the time I got there I was past caring'. All together her labour lasted 29 hours and she had to have an episiotomy at the final stage of delivery – totally against her ideal birth. There were no signs of any problems with the baby during labour but:

> As soon as his head popped out – he had swallowed his own waste matter. C [her community midwife] suctioned him out and then sent for a paediatrician. Then he was born. I was hardly able to hold him because they wanted to resuscitate him. His breathing was a bit peculiar so I wasn't able to breastfeed him. I literally held him for seconds – then they took him and suctioned him even more.

Then the baby was admitted to the special care unit (SCBU), and it was discovered that the suctioning had been too vigorous and he had suffered a collapsed lung. Lynn and her husband were able to visit the SCBU any time, but they could not hold their son as he was in an incubator with 'lots of monitors'. Lynn considered that she took the whole thing calmly at the time – but mainly because she was so tired. 'I never thought about brain damage or anything like that. I just said "is he going to be alright?" and they said "oh yes"'.

Lynn was discharged. As she lived very near the

hospital (5 minutes' drive), she didn't see much problem in not being able to hold her baby and had not planned to be in hospital anyway. Her parents immediately came to stay and looked after her, and she herself recovered physically very quickly. However, the SCBU was very full at the time and they wanted to discharge Lynn's baby to the postnatal-care ward once they considered he was fit enough. Normally the mother would have been on the ward, and 'enormous pressure' was put on Lynn to be admitted so the baby could be there with her. However, she believed that she would find it difficult to cope in the hospital, because she knew she needed the constant support of both her husband and parents:

> *I just refused. Maybe I was really awful. I know I wouldn't have been good going in – it wouldn't have been good for him or me. They do have some bedrooms for parents but they were all occupied. So they put him in the nursery of the postnatal ward. Then we went to visit him in the nursery – we thought it would be a place with a few babies and staff. But their so-called nursery was basically the storeroom where they kept the baby bath and scales. He was there on his own and a nurse popped in every 4 hours. And the reason they wanted him in was to keep him under observation!*

Getting the best support over the postnatal period

The family made a fuss and took the baby home with them. This had been very upsetting for Lynn, and she felt relieved on arriving home as she could look after the baby and be well supported. This didn't stop her being very tired. 'What I have found – although everyone says "it's a full time job" – is that until it happens, no one can convey, this is a 24-hour full-time job!' What saved her from getting overwrought and down was that she was not left on her own. Her parents, grandmother and husband took it in turns to help with all but the breastfeeding. 'I'm now in the 5th week and I have constant support – and I've needed that.' The worst thing was:

> I think just the sheer tiredness. It was feed, nappy, feed, nappy. I've been absolutely exhausted. My grandmother came down early because I decided that I could not do 2 days on my own. I think [why she didn't get depressed] it's not being alone. Someone else to hold him, someone else to change nappies and someone else to ensure that **you** eat. My mum said she had had someone with her for 5 weeks as well.

Because things were going so well, Lynn managed to go to a work-related conference with her father (to help with the baby) and one or two meetings which made her feel good.

Lynn felt that, apart from the constant support of her family, the support of C, the community midwife, was another crucial element. The midwife not only supported her and guided her with things like breast-feeding, but re-assured her about the baby's continuing health following the earlier scare. At the subsequent meetings we had, Lynn was clearly going from strength to strength.

I have placed Lynn and Jerri's case side by side to show how important the way a trauma surrounding birth is handled can be for future maternal well-being.

Jerri's maternity care was insensitive to her particular needs, and there was even an attempt to deprive her of her partner's support at a vital stage. Lynn was supported throughout even though her 'worst fear' of having to go to hospital was realised, and she was very upset over the baby's health and welfare. She had her husband and midwife to support and advise her on these matters, which made all the difference. The midwife, in particular, was able to ensure that she had support when trying to confront the hospital regime.

Lynn was also far luckier in her family background – not only because they provided excellent support over the first 5 weeks, but because they all liked each other and this clearly was representative of her early childhood history too.

Coping with depressed moods

No one I spoke to managed to get through the postnatal months without feeling down, fed up or, in some cases, really disressed at times. The incidents they told me about were significant enough to stand out in their memory as *distinct from their normal day-to-day selves*, even in their new situation as mothers. They were examples of the postnatal distress and depressed moods experienced by around 70% of new mothers. If these feelings of distress are not separated by periods of calm, then they might lead to a serious clinical depression.

For example, Jane loved her baby. When I visited her when the baby was 3 months old, she took obvious pleasure from bouncing her on her lap and smiling into her eyes. However, she told me she had felt seriously depressed for a week or two when her daughter was about 6 weeks old:

She [the baby] did have a time when she was pretty grotty and that got me down ... when her teeth were down but still coming through. She whined all during the day – when I wanted to go out and get things done. She whined and wouldn't sleep. She wanted you to carry her and stand up all the time. There was nothing I could give her.

This time passed and the day-to-day events that might be a bit frustrating were not in themselves significant enough to cause her any serious distress. I asked Jane how she was looking after *herself*. She was worried that she was neglecting her appearance – she didn't have time for the make-up, hair or nail routines that she had previously enjoyed. However, she thought she was managing the house reasonably well. What she missed the most was her social life. However, her fiancé of 4 years (with whom she lived) continued *his* social life once the early childcare stage was over. He would stay out late and bring his friends round to the house – either way it would be difficult for Jane, who felt excluded and exploited. He loved the baby, but took it for granted that she should do all the nappy changing, feeding, cooking and house-work. Jane was finding herself without any social support. Not only did she have to cope with the tasks she had, but she also had to make decisions relating to the baby's welfare – a responsibility that she would have preferred to share. The friends who did come to visit seemed to expect both Jane and her fiancé to have returned to (what they saw as) normal – that is, the way they were before they became parents. It was easier for her partner to do that. He could put on a front to his friends, but this left Jane feeling abandoned, exploited by their friends and taken for granted by her fiancé.

Finding social support

Luckily, Jane managed to make friends with other women in her situation, and one in particular (a mother of twins of similar age to her daughter), who lived nearby, became a close friend. It was the support of this friend that prevented some of the problems she faced gaining the upper hand over her emotional state and precipitating depression.

Social scientists, who have been carrying out research in the area of motherhood and PND, have demonstrated time and again that a major factor that leads to a woman's vulnerability to PND is *lack of social support*. Their research has identified the gap between two popular myths. They are, first, that all women find motherhood 'natural' and therefore easy, and, second, that being at home and looking after a young baby is all about having a good social life with other mothers and spending time on yourself. Being a full-time housebound mother can be one of the loneliest occupations in the world. Having responsibility for a baby means not being able to get out and meet people without a great deal of effort. It means putting the needs of others before your own every time. It also means, for many women, that they need to find new ways of being social with others. If you've only ever made friends at work or through social activities – where people are available to get to know – how do you meet people who, like yourself, find it difficult to get out of the house? Jane was lucky because her new friend lived nearby and they saw each other in the park on more than one occasion. Jane forced herself to talk because it was clear they were in similar boats. Even then she was lucky they liked each other.

Social support, then, is about not feeling isolated because you share things with someone else. It is also about having access to someone who can help you out, when you need it, with advice, babysitting, getting some shopping or just being available to talk to when another adult voice can help. What might appear to be support does not always work that way, though.

Not all company is supportive

Norma had had a previous history of a serious clinical depression for which she had had psychiatric outpatient treatment. She was, therefore, particularly sensitised to ensuring that she did not have a similar postnatal experience. The first few weeks were very difficult for her and she would get periods of extreme frustration and distress. Initially, after her son was born, she felt herself besieged by visitors and well-wishers:

> *I had so many visitors. It's the one thing I regret – that people just kept dropping in! Just sort of acquaintances. At one stage I cried. They were just talking to each other and I didn't have a night-dress on. I said 'would you mind leaving the room please' and I went to the toilet and just sat there for an hour crying. I felt the toilet was the only room that people couldn't come and get me.*

Norma, who was a midwife herself as were some of her friends, found that everyone kept offering her advice. This was particularly related to breastfeeding, and most of them thought she was making a rod for her own back because her baby always seemed hungry:

*I got really angry. I couldn't believe how angry I got. I knew before he was born people would give me advice – but the only person who **didn't** give me advice was my midwife. She just said 'whatever you're doing you're doing it right'. One friend of mine who is a midwife disturbed me so much I lost my temper and threw her out. She took him from me, walked him up and down and tried to put his thumb in his mouth. He got into a dreadful state. Then she wouldn't let me pick him up. My hair was standing on end. Eli [her husband] was out and I started to cry!*

Looking back, Norma believed it was the tiredness, following the pain and 'strange' experience that childbirth seemed to represent, that had got to her more than anything. The other thing she found distressing was when Eli had to return to work. 'Nothing got done – I had no time to eat until Eli arrived home and cooked dinner. The baby wouldn't settle – he needed feeding all the time.

One day, she found herself really miserable and feeling that she needed to 'get away', so they went to visit her sister who lived in the country. On the way there, she realised that she had spent all the time shouting at Eli and she had been doing so ever since the baby had been born. She realised that he must be getting fed up, and, when she thought about it, recognised not only her extreme tiredness but that she had never had time to herself – and she could only vent her frustrations upon Eli:

It's been more difficult than I thought it would be. It's not being able to do anything. Not even to put the washing in the washing machine or cook a meal except when Eli's here.

When I visited Norma for the last time, though, she had secured herself a part-time midwife post and a local child-minder. 'Things have more or less fallen into place. I'm really happy. Absolutely. Things have worked out so well.'

Norma and Eli had a strong relationship and he was prepared to weather the storm with her. He knew about her previous experiences of depression and realised that she might get distressed. However, he found it hard. Norma herself had enough insight to realise what was happening to her and then to their relationship. It was also important to Norma to find time to think about what was happening to her and realise that she was distressed and depressed because of a series of experiences all of which followed the long and tiring labour. Having friends 'in the business' clearly did not help – they wanted to advise her rather than support (in contrast to *her* midwife). She herself had a clear investment, as a professional midwife, in being seen to handle the birth and postnatal weeks 'perfectly'. The result was that she felt overwhelmed by what *she thought* was her own inability and the pressure from friends. Her friends clearly did not see her as the strong, independent and competent person she was usually.

Getting support to prevent PND

Sharon had been brought up to be self-reliant. She had been to a boarding school and spent a year as an au pair in Australia before settling down to her marriage, where she had been in charge of the running of the home and social life for her businessman husband. Sharon developed a good social-support network. She knew that her businessman husband would have little time to be helpful in a practical way, but they could afford to have someone to help with household duties and a cleaner to allow her to concentrate on baby care for the first few weeks. She also ensured that she maintained the good contacts she had developed while she was pregnant.

Sharon prided herself on *avoiding* 'the postnatal depression period', by ensuring that seeking support prevented any feelings that she might be heading for depression. She was fortunate in being involved with a good postnatal support group, which ran classes organised by the NCT:

The postnatal class was a terrific help! The girl who took the classes was really good – you went along – she's a trained – something to do with children ... She came into hospital and she knew what she was talking about. I went to the postnatal classes and it was wonderful listening to other people's problems. There was always somebody with a worse problem than you. I felt the postnatal class helped me tremendously. But she just gave me that boost.

It was a great help to be able to talk about problems such as sore nipples, a routine, the day-to-day problems. For example, if you can't get out of the house, you sit and think 'my God! I'm the only one with these problems'. If you can't talk about it to anyone – it's a disaster. It's what starts dragging you down – which is where your postnatal depression might appear. Because you literally get depressed about everything.

Yes, I was very lucky as there was always someone at the other end of the phone to speak to about it and I'd seem to have a list of all the right

phone numbers and everyone I spoke to was terrific-
ally re-assuring and calmed me down, and I feel I
owe them an awful lot. When girlfriends now have
their first babies I can see how much friends help. I
might sound awfully pompous about it but I feel
there's so much I could tell them. I wish people
*had told **me** beforehand.*

To prevent episodes of depression joining up, you have to
be either lucky (which you can't do much about) or stra-
tegic (which you can). There are always other people
having a baby around the same time as you. Try to talk
to people at antenatal clinics and classes. Find out whether
there are special groups for postnatal support in your area,
before you have the baby. Not everyone can afford help
around the house but many have parents, siblings and
friends. Plan in advance what you would like them to
do. Lynn managed to do this. Gwen, whose mother
came to stay for the two weeks after the birth, ended by
asking her mother to leave. Her mother did not know what
to do to help and took the opportunity to talk to Gwen,
play with the baby and drink 'endless cups of tea'. Gwen
wanted the cleaning, shopping and cooking to be done. It
might have worked out better for both of them if she had
been clear about that in advance.

What has happened to me?

As the stories above show, there are lots of *individual*
reasons why women get depressed after childbirth. There
are also reasons that many women *share*. One constant time
of vulnerability seems to be the lull after the storm. Once
the immediate impact of all the stress, pain, anxiety,

surprise, congratulations and joy are at a standstill and routine returns, you begin to wonder 'what about *me?*' 'What *happened* to me?' These feelings come about because the excitement has died down. Also, there is a wide gap between the 'self' prior to pregnancy and the person you have become a year or so down the line. Sometimes, this can be confusing simply because it is difficult to recapture the parts of your former self that you most valued. You fear that you are no longer that person. When you feel like this, it is difficult to realise that things will change *yet again* beyond recognition, when the baby is more independent, when you have *adapted to the developments and changes* that the baby has made to your life.

Angela had had her second son. Her husband Mark was a lorry driver who worked mainly at night, which meant he was around during the day to give her support. They were not particularly well off financially when Angela was not working, but they could 'manage'. Both her parents, her brother and sister and his family lived nearby and both Angela and Mark had been brought up locally. There were plenty of opportunities for support. Angela had had a history of severe depression, which led to her making an almost fatal suicide attempt. Underlying that depression was a sense of extreme loss. She had had an earlier career working undercover for the police, which was her life. 'It's a job that totally preoccupies you. You don't think about anything else really.' She believed that it had necessarily made her into a hard and cynical person, almost without her realising that it had happened. Listening to what she said also gave an indication as to why she fell so hard into her depression when the trigger came:

Angela: *The biggest thing is not trusting anyone – anyone at all. You're way too suspicious of any* *circumstance – you think there is something more to a situation than there is. You read more into things – you're always thinking of the bad things – that's what you associate people with. I think that's probably why you become so cynical. You think that people are trying to get one over on you all the time because they know what you are and you think 'Oh, I've got to be one step ahead!' and if you're not that way to start with, it must be a strain. I couldn't stand it any more [after 10 years] – it was driving me really barmy.*

Paula: *So – after you'd stopped, how long did it take to return to normal – or haven't you yet?*

Angela: *Well just about. Basically – I'm worried when I'm in the street that I'm going to be mugged – which I didn't have before, as I had this false confidence thinking I could stop this happening. Now – I won't go out on my own – I'm frightened to.*

Her view of the world (whether it was one she had always held or one that came from working for the police) was almost a 'manufactured' depressive perspective – isolation, mistrust, not seeing any good and being suspicious if something looked as if it were, feeling the world is against you and dangerous. The development of this world view seemed both essential and inevitable to Angela. All this on top of what was hard work. She had only left the force four years before the first interview. But the pain and fear were still there. Angela felt that, over the past few years since she had been living with Mark and had had her first child two years previously, she had mostly cut loose from that perspective and the friends she had had. Although it was in some ways a relief, it was also a major part of herself that had disappeared:

Paula: *So the last two or three years you've had a much greater change in your life than a lot of women?*

Angela: *Yes – amazing. I still sit and think I don't believe I've got here. Particularly, the last years before I left were very turbulent – job wise and personal-wise, – relationship-wise. To think I've settled down and become a housewife amazes me – also a lot of my friends say – 'I never thought you'd end up like this'.*

Paula: *Do you keep in touch with old colleagues?*

Angela: *No it just shows you – a girl I was very close to – I haven't spoken to her since – gosh! – since Jeremy was a baby – two years. It's difficult – you don't have anything in common any more – I find that I still kept in touch when I first had Jeremy. I went to a few police 'dos' – but I felt totally out of it. I had no experiences to relate to them – and a lot of their humour, I found just wasn't me. I found it very strange they weren't interested in my being married and that I had a little baby – because that was the biggest thing in my life. Then – and I couldn't understand why it wasn't important to them – as friends of mine. But I wasn't interested earlier when others had left and had babies.*

Angela's change of identity was particularly dramatic because, at the time married women and mothers could not do active duty in her line of work. However, she left the force prior to living with Mark because her life took a turn for the worse. She had been having a relationship for five years with a married police officer and the strain of everything began to catch up with her. She couldn't cope with the job and the relationship anymore because she was fully involved in both and felt she was fast losing control over her life:

Angela: *I took an overdose, which was stupid.*

Paula: *When you felt so bad – could you see anything at all good in the future?*

Angela: *I couldn't – no I couldn't see an end. It was going round and round and nothing was getting solved, and I just didn't have the foresight to stop it. I didn't see any way of getting out. I think it was more a cry for help than waiting to kill myself. No – I thought – I didn't want to keep going on like this. My mum and dad were going through a bad patch too – they had their trouble. I don't think that was helping either – They got over theirs – eventually. I think that if you don't have the stability – I felt I couldn't bother my parents – so it was just my two friends and once I'd been in hospital – that really pulled me together – the shock of what I'd done. And I felt a policewoman is supposed to have control of my own and other people's lives. I'd made a total shambles of my own. That was it – but then once I'd come out, I thought I had to do something.*

After that, Angela left the force and had to fight depression and loneliness until she met Mark, and they began to build a life together. However, she was depressed after Jeremy was born and felt that mildly paranoid feelings crept up on her:

Angela: *I can remember talking about this the other day – I said 'do you remember what I was like,' and he said 'I remember that you'd jump at the slightest thing, and your temper was really short – but he didn't remember with me having a go at him all the time. But he would have been preoccupied with Jeremy as everything was such an effort – I'd go on and moan at Mark, which wasn't like me at all.*

Paula: *Do you remember how it felt when it started to come on?*

Angela: *Feelings of insecurity again – not feeling safe. I remember feeling – that he'd been doing nightwork since I was pregnant with Jeremy – and for some reason I thought – it's easy for him to be seeing someone else, and not working. Things I'd never dreamt of before. I don't know where it had come from – that's why it's so confusing, 'cos you don't know why you're feeling like this – and crying like that for no reason. It came on all of a sudden – it seems such a long time ago – I was very weepy after I'd had Jeremy, but then that didn't bother me. Everything was fine – we got back to normal, our sex life was good – and all of a sudden – it went wrong. I didn't feel happy with myself. I had lost a lot of weight to get married, and I've*

always been overweight – and I kept a lot of it
after I had Jeremy. I put on 3 stone when I was
pregnant.

Angela's feelings about her safety and self-confidence,
which had become stronger since leaving the police and
recovering from her first depression, seemed to return
following the aftermath of childbirth. She told me that
she had felt ashamed of her performance during
Jeremy's birth, as she had not coped well with the pain.
She was particularly upset because, despite her best
efforts, the whole delivery had been out of her control.
For Angela 'shame' was a major factor in her self-
esteem. She had felt so ashamed when she recovered
from the overdose. She felt shame when she lost control
in front of the midwives and was ashamed of her body,
which again had appeared to get 'out of control'. She had
rarely felt isolated from friends or family, but had not
found that talking about her problems to them necessarily
helped. That was the reason she volunteered to meet with
me during the second pregnancy.

She was far more satisfied with herself after Carey's
birth. Although he had been in some distress during the
birth (the cord was around his neck), she felt she had
responded well to what was required of her and they
were both fine. It was very important for Angela to feel
she knew what she was doing and could do it with the
minimum of help:

There was a girl in the delivery room next to me
doing what I did first time – I could hear her. I
said I felt really sorry for her – I knew just what
she was going through, you could hear them all
telling her what to do.

The early days, on returning home, were enjoyable although hard work with the two young children (Jeremy was still under 2). However, once Mark returned to work, she felt a sense of social isolation return because although he was at home during the day:

> *I'm very lucky because I have him at home during the day and then my mum comes round in the evening for a couple of hours so I'm not really on my own. But it can be frustrating in other ways with Mark being at home. Whereas everybody else – my friends have a normal routine. Their husbands are out during the day so they can get to see friends – I can't do that. I'm stuck here. I have to get Mark up – or else he'll just sleep all day. I have to be here to wake him up – and then we have dinner at 4.00 – so at 2.00 I'm thinking about cooking dinner – so really I can't get out and see friends.*
>
> *So in one way it has advantages – but also drawbacks. I sometimes think I'd really like to get out and see my friends – but I can't. They come to me – but I feel the need to get away from my own surroundings.*
>
> *Often I sit here – and think – 'oh I wish someone would pop in a have a glass of wine or something!' but people don't. Their kids are in bed – or they're going out themselves.*

Despite the good social-support network, Angela felt frustrated and a bit trapped for other reasons – her routine conflicted with that of her peers. This isolated her. Other things bothered he too. She stopped breast-feeding Carey because he never seemed to get enough milk. Bottle-feeding had the great advantage of both

Angela and Mark being able to take turns, she didn't
suffer from sore nipples and Carey slept for reasonable
amounts of time between feeds. However:

Paula: *After you stopped – how did you feel?*

Angela: *Upset – and I still felt guilty and every
time I was feeding him [with a bottle] – I kept
wanting to go back to it [breastfeeding]. There
are times when I still want to put him there –
but I haven't. I think once you've made a
decision to break you should break. If there's
still milk there you can start again. I was in
two minds whether to do that. He had settled
a bit better – but that was because of the bottle –
he was so hungry. He was so content – and I
thought if I put him back – he'll still need the
bottle and I shall get him in a state and it's not
worth it.*

Angela lacked confidence in her childcare skills. She had
decided to bottle-feed and the results were positive, but
she was nagged by guilt and the temptation and desire to
breastfeed.

The third meeting I had with Angela found her
satisfied with the development and care she and Mark
could give to both children. Her worry at this stage was
to *return to being herself.* She was looking for a typing post,
but without a great deal of success.

*I've been trying to get back to work. I've got Mark
home in the day – and there've been a few jobs
going. I want to get back with typing – I don't*

want to waste my skills. I've got very resentful of being turned down because of having young children. Once it wasn't said to me – but another one said he was worried that I had young children. It annoys me they won't even let you put your side of it.

I found it hard – I'm frightened I'm going to end up cleaning or stacking shelves in a supermarket because I know that's a job – but I want to use the skills I've got – I don't want to lose my typing.

I think I'd had a bad day recently (I was talking to my friend). I said 'when you become a housewife you virtually have an operation to have your brain removed!' You just become like a vegetable.

I found it hard filling in forms – going back to schooldays – what qualifications I've got. For the first couple I found it hard to sit and think about things, other than children and shopping lists. That I resent!

This kind of experience is common to many women, particularly those without high-level formal qualifications or those who have successfully managed to work in a way that is not compatible with having young children. The last time I met Angela, when Carey was 6 months old, she had applied for several posts, none of which she had got. She was very upset and becoming worried about financial strains as well as issues of identity. She felt ambivalent towards motherhood now, which she expressed more clearly than she had before. She still pined for her identity as a police officer (even though it was not that that she had given up for motherhood, but a typing job) 'when people did what you told them to do'.

This she laughed was very different from her husband and children's reaction! She found several of the other mothers she knew difficult to get on with, because they had not 'led independent lives'. She felt she would be 'quite happy to have less responsibility for the children and let Mark take over'. Even so she felt she might try and have another child, a girl if she could, because she was unable to find suitable employment.

Angela was probably the person who had the most complicated relationship to her emotional and psychological state. She was very reflexive and particularly interested in talking to me about her feelings and what they indicated. She spent a great deal of time analysing why she was the way she was, particularly because her personality and professional background were so different from those of her friends. She was well supported, but isolated because of her difference. Also, as she was essentially working class and did not have a formal education, she was also isolated from other women who had (or continued to hold) responsible and interesting jobs. For Angela then, her self-esteem had developed from the things that attracted her into her police career and the process of that work. It gave her a great sense of power, autonomy and difference. However, it also meant she was isolated and distrustful, and, when faced with an emotional crisis, she had no way of drawing upon her own resources or seeking support because of her sense of personal shame. It was this shame at not being 'perfect' and in control that also made her vulnerable at time during the delivery of her first son. It was the lack of recognition she experienced, for being a person in her own right, that led to her bouts of feeling down becoming longer and more severe. It was the fact that her husband and parents were so supportive that ensured that she managed to function as a mother and *communicate* her distress.

Motherhood and the arrival of self-confidence

Melanie, also married to a lorry driver, was in a very different position. Both she and her husband were middle class and well educated. She had a well-paid professional job and it was her husband who was going to give up work and take major responsibility for childcare. Melanie had come out of a failed marriage and a consequent period of depression, when she met John her present husband. 'I had tended to see my house as a prison for a while. I went in and shut all the doors and windows.'

After the birth of their daughter, Melanie tried in vain to breastfeed and could not. This had a positive side as it meant that the couple were able to share all the early weeks of infant care – feeding, changing and looking after the home. Thus, although both were tired, neither was totally exhausted or felt exploited:

> *I think the wisest thing we ever did was to cope on our own and not to involve anyone else. No mums running in and out. We didn't want them in the beginning ... if we didn't know what was wrong, we would get the book out. It was something we did together rather than just listening. I'm glad we did it the way we did.*

After three months' leave, Melanie returned to work. She believed that being a mother had made her a happier and more contented person than she had been before:

> *Someone said the other day 'Gosh it suits you!' I know exactly what they mean but I can't put it into*

words. Now I'm more confident. I came home from work the other day and thought 'God I'm ambitious now' ... I'm the provider and I must do well for the family.

Melanie experienced a strange paradox in that 'I've never been more tired – but never had so much energy!' She had not lost her identity and her self-esteem not only remained well intact, but the extra sense of responsibility and power infused her with pleasure and energy.

Happiness and loss: the paradox of PND

Introduction

> *Parenthood is a seething pit of paradox ... The biggest contradiction of all is that motherhood is a shockingly lovely state, yet childcare is a spectacularly ghastly activity. We're not supposed to admit it. Recently, however, I've taken to blurted confessions. People are startled.*[1]

This paradox is at the very heart of PND. It takes insight, support, inner strength and a well-nurtured self-esteem to acknowledge to your*self* that the happiness of being a mother is counterbalanced by the problems of the motherhood role. The extent to which you have emotional and psychological difficulties with the role depend very much on how much support you have, your financial situation, accommodation and other practical and material aspects of life. It also depends upon your expectations and fantasies about life as a mother, as Betty Friedan illustrates:

*It was a strange stirring, a sense of dissatisfaction,
a yearning that women suffered in the middle of the
twentieth century in the United States. Each sub-
urban wife struggled with it alone. As she made the
beds, shopped for groceries, matched slip cover
material, ate peanut butter sandwiches with her
children, chauffeured Cub Scouts and Brownies,
lay beside her husband at night, she was afraid to
ask, even of herself, the silent question: 'is this
all?'*[2]

Hannah Gavron and Ann Oakley,[3] among several others,
have also written detailed and disturbing accounts of the
social conditions that surround the day-to-day existence
of women who have young children. Gavron's study suggested that this cuts across social-class groups. She found
that expectations of marriage and motherhood appeared
to be at odds with the actual experience. This led to
confusion surrounding women's roles:

*For some wives of both classes marriage was seen as
a kind of freedom; yet when it was combined with
motherhood it became a kind of prison and they felt
their freedom had been restricted before they had
really been free at all*[4].

Whether they are mostly at home or in full or part-time
employment, the burdens of childcare and household
management fall upon their shoulders. For almost all
women, this means that motherhood (the gain) is accompanied by a change in circumstances (usually a loss or
series of losses). Ann Oakley had found a pattern of
disillusion among the mothers she interviewed. She suggested that while marriage and motherhood are expected

to provide the greatest life satisfaction for women, in reality they provide disappointment. Women without children frequently have a highly romanticised picture of motherhood and '. . . before motherhood is experienced they want more children than they do later'[5]. Mothers lose their dream and with it part of their self.

The experience of loss

Loss is a core concept in the development of the human psyche. Psychologists have made the case for the importance of emotional *attachment* to human emotional *strength* ever since Freud's work on bereavement at the end of the 19th century. He was one of the first thinkers who influenced contemporary thought to suggest that the expression of grief following bereavement was not only natural and acceptable, but highly desirable. It was important to cry. It was important *not* to maintain the Victorian stiff upper lip. To bury such fundamental feelings of anguish would distort recovery and prevent emotional healing. The loss would be buried in the unconscious and never resolved. Some of the after-effects would be similar to what we now think of as PTSD (post-traumatic stress disorder) discussed in Chapter 3. There is a difference between looking back at a period of mourning with sadness and even shedding a tear for the lost person, and having intrusive thoughts and dreams which cause anxiety. The latter is symptomatic of unresolved grief.

It is not only bereavement that leads to grief. Peter Marris[6] has shown that moving away from home and changes in the structure of a community can lead to a grief reaction. I myself have done research on the experience of being burgled and discovered that this too can, in some cases, lead to a severe grief reaction, particularly if someone has lost items of great sentimental value or feel their once-loved house has 'let them down'.

Motherhood routinely leads a woman to have a series of losses. These losses need to be acknowledged and mourned. Grief following a loss in any other context is socially acceptable. It is frequently encouraged, as nowadays most people realise that the process of grief leads to a healthy recovery. This does not mean that the person forgets what they have lost. They manage to integrate their feelings of loss into their view of the world and their self-image.

The opportunity for grief in postnatal women seems to be unacceptable. The paradox is that women do experience severe loss as they become mothers (each time). They lose:

- sleep;
- time to themselves;
- a sense of personal independence;
- their self-esteem;
- belief in their abilities;
- the shape and usual feelings from their bodies;
- their sexuality;
- their occupation;
- money;
- friends;
- patterns of relationships at home and elsewhere; and
- underlying these losses – their identity, a fundamental recognition of who they really are.

These losses are not all permanent, although some may be, but they are integral to the experience of becoming a mother.

The healthy grief reaction involves *recognition of the losses* – Some people deny their loss – even when it involves the break-up of a marriage for instance, or children leaving home – because they feel it helps them 'deal' with the problem. Many people do not want to acknowledge their emotional responses, even to themselves, because they see them as a sign of weakness. These people bury their feelings, but feelings so fundamental as the response to loss do not go away that easily. The anomaly of seeing yourself as having experienced loss at the same time as becoming a mother is painful for many women. It is not widely acknowledged. Indeed, if you try to look up information about 'loss and childbirth' or 'loss and motherhood' on any academic literature search, the results will show 'miscarriage' or 'stillbirth'. The literature about loss does not relate to successful childbirth. And yet, there is a great deal of loss for women around this time.

The healthy grief reaction

John Archer,[7] an expert on the evolution of human emotions and behaviour, has studied human expressions of grief. From his examination of the research evidence, he describes the typical grief reaction. Most of the research he describes was about bereavement in widowhood, but he also looked at some other studies where a similar kind of response could be found:

1 There is the *numbness and disbelief*, which is seen as a psychological defence against the extreme pain. The individual denies they are feeling such grief or represses it. If this stage lasts, then there is likely to be a psychological repercussion of, say, unexplained and prolonged depression. For new mothers, the exhaustion and carrying out infant-care tasks is a physical means of numbness. You get on with the tasks without thinking. If you think too hard about what is happening, you might resent the baby, your partner or friends.

2 The second response to grief, which sometimes follows the numbness is also a form of denial, is an *expression of anger*. This sometimes happens when a few weeks have passed and you are on your own. Anger might overcome you because of your partner's return to work or your friends' lack of sustained interest in your stories about the baby or your own ability to manage everything as you used to do.

3 This may be followed by *guilt and self-blame* as the third characteristic of a grief reaction.

4 *Distress and anxiety* often accompany much of the bereaved person's behaviour, which Colin Murray Parkes,[8] in his description of early widowhood, depicted as anxiety verging on panic. This will include sobbing, hyperventilation, inability to sleep, restlessness and psychosomatic problems such as eczema.

5 Bereavement leads to *yearning and preoccupation* with what has been lost – 'pining' is a word that well describes an aspect of this state. After that, bereaved people sometimes *hallucinate or dream* about their lost state of being or the person. The process often ends in a *depression* which is an

important precursor to the *acceptance of the loss*. It means that the person is facing and experiencing the pain of grief having recognised its reality. They no longer try to avoid the pain and only once they see the loss for what it really is are they able to accept it and rebuild their lives.

Archer argues that this is not only a process that can be seen in humans living in sophisticated societies – there are many studies of primitive communities of humans and studies of primates that demonstrate that such grief is a universal, and evolutionary and thus adaptive process. In other words, it happens whether we like it or not. It is part of the natural way of assisting our emotional healing.

Knowledge of the common features of grief reactions, following more frequently recognised experiences of loss, have led psychologists to show that there are both successful and pathological outcomes for the process. Some people continue to grieve for years, which can result in embittered ruined lives. Some people react by expressing their anger, and there are always stories of people who commit murder if they believe someone has been responsible for the break-up of their relationship or the death of their loved one.

There is no clear pathway to 'getting over' loss. However, the major factor in psychological adjustment and reintegration is the *acceptance of loss and that things have changed*. Another major factor is to recognise where blame (if any) lies and not to take it all upon yourself.

In order to recover from the paradoxical losses surrounding motherhood, you need to recognise they are there. Following that, the psychological effort needs to be in re-building your sense of who you are while integrating the changes. So what are the losses and how might they affect you?

Losing sleep

Everyone I spoke to had some experience of this. The
first, most obvious and perhaps the most underestimated
loss is the loss of sleep. Everyone expressed their tiredness
and few predicted how tired they would actually be. But
lack of sleep has a psychological and physiological impact
on health – it affects your judgement, it makes you
irritable, it prevents you dreaming, which psychologists
agree is vital for mental health, it impacts upon your
eating habits and digestive system and has a negative
effect upon memory, ability to make decisions, sex drive
and also self-esteem. Thus even if there was no baby to
look after, home to run and other tasks to perform, sleep
deprivation in itself is guaranteed to make you feel pretty
dreadful. However, it is clear that, from what women say
about the early weeks and months of motherhood, there is
a lot to do when you are awake! Thus losing sleep means
that you are very busy while being in a mental and
physical state, which really means you are not up to the
job! No employer would accept you turning up for work
following weeks of broken sleep. You would not be considered fit for work. While many mothers do not have a
choice – they have to carry on – it does not mean that you
are strange to feel angry and resentful that you are not
getting the sleep you need. It is a vicious circle – which
leaves you little time to reflect – you are exhausted and
irritable because you have lost so much sleep. You are
angry that you are sleep-deprived.

Almost all the women I spoke to saw tiredness as being
a trigger for getting particularly down, and catching up on
some sleep as being helpful. Sylvia, for example, said
'Depression – that's when you get overtired. If I get
tired, I get irritable. I get miserable and then I get

depressed. But usually a good night's sleep solves the problem a little.'

Meg described herself as not getting depressed so much as:

> *just completely knackered! Sometimes my husband spots it quicker than me. He'll say 'you need to go to bed love' ... but **I** don't always spot it. Actually what happens is that I start turning on Brian and saying 'it's not fair. You just don't do enough around the house.' He'll say 'you need to go to bed early.' I'll say 'grrrr'. But he's right.*

The important message in Meg's example is not the rights or wrongs of who does the most work, but the need to recognise that becoming a mother does not mean a woman has to sacrifice her sleep and health all of the time. She needs to be aware of her needs (and wants) and to ensure that others respect that. A difficult task, of course, but one that forms the essential basis to *recognition that things have changed* in a permanent way. Failure to act upon this and ignore your own needs is a denial of the losses and changes and fuels resentment.

Losing time

Losing sleep and its consequences leads to a loss of time to yourself – to reflect, to have some fun, to spend time on your appearance, your health needs, talking to friends and being with your partner without the trammels of household duties getting in the way. Again, there are psychological and physical consequences of not having time in this way. Some is about the lack of time to reflect and understand where you are in the scheme of things in relation to your family, your past and future. In the grieving process, it is this reflection than enables the re-integration that Peter Marris[6] talks about. Reflection allows you to recall yourself in the past before the loss (e.g. as a wife), and move on towards understanding and coping with yourself as a widow. Grieving is the bridge that links you and ensures your identity is maintained even though you might 'fall into little pieces' and feel 'shattered' by your loss. Grief and mourning are legitimate for widows. They are not so for new mothers.

There is not time to mourn. Thus you lose touch with who you are more sharply than if you were alone, crying and thinking. That sounds paradoxical. To be alone and morose appears to be exactly what the new mother wants to avoid. Not only because of the social expectation of happiness. It is your own expectation as well. All that seems to have happened is that you have a baby. There's nothing in that event on its own to cry about – unless we give it a label: PND. This crying then becomes symp-tomatic of an illness or disorder.

If the depression and grief do not get resolved bit by bit after the loss following widowhood or divorce, then there may well be mental-health problems that need further attention. Likewise, with new mothers.

However, with new mothers the opportunity for grief is denied to them – because of social taboos. But, while it may seem awful to you to cry 'I wish I never had had this baby', it might be more acceptable to cry 'I wish I could have some time to sleep' and 'I am so upset that I cannot spend time alone doing my own thing'. As Hilary said 'I have re-adjusted what I consider time to myself. I suppose I've lowered my definition of what that really means.'

Bodies

Our bodies are always a main concern in our lives. Bodies need to be healthy and fit in order to cope. To cope with childbirth, breastfeeding, infant care and household management requires enormous amounts of energy, stamina and strength. In addition, we want our bodies to be attractive – not only to others but perhaps most importantly to ourselves.

Pregnancy changes the body's shape. It also brings about physical changes which may lead to problems. Being pregnant means that the body you knew and had learned to live with is no longer there. Kate Mosse,[9] the writer, describes her experience of pregnancy:

> *on the surface I appeared to be the same woman. I couldn't shake off the sense of how dangerous and unnatural it all was. Having always trusted my body and my instincts, I woke every morning convinced that something was wrong.*

From pregnancy onwards, something is being taken away from you – your familiarity with your own body. From that time, others are given the kind of access to your body that they would not have at any other time. You are told 'you are pregnant – you are not ill'. And yet, what happens is that you come under the thumb of health professionals.

Esther Rantzen, on her BBC TV programme *That's Life*, commissioned a survey of over 6,000 women during pregnancy, childbirth and early motherhood. It showed that a significant number of pregnant women had disliked the antenatal care they received in hospital, and the antenatal clinics were described as 'cattlemarkets'. From the first antenatal appointment, we get a sneak preview of how motherhood is valued and mothers are treated. The uniqueness of your own pregnancy, and expectations and desires for the baby you are carrying, don't coincide with the views and responses of health professionals you meet. Decisions are made for you. You spend a great deal of time waiting to see midwives and doctors. Procedures are not explained clearly. Your body is invaded, sometimes painfully. You may be treated discourteously and sometimes things happen to you to which you don't recall having consented.

Once the baby is born though, this doesn't go away. The health-care professionals are less invasive once they have established that 'all is well' – but their concerns are not the same as yours.

Many women suffer a great deal of pain for weeks and sometimes months after the birth, particularly if they have had a vaginal delivery and the perineum has torn or there had been a larger than average episiotomy wound. This is sometimes true for Caesarean deliveries too.

Matilda had had a long and painful labour, which ended in an unplanned Caesarean operation:

> *After the operation I had a tremendous amount of pain. They didn't give me any painkillers after. It was just as if they were still cutting ... They said 'are you going to feed her?' I said 'OK', but they had to do almost everything for me. I couldn't even lift her myself.*

When Matilda came out of hospital:

> *There was a swelling along the stitches and I had a lot of pain. They had got me infected. So the doctor*

gave me some cream and eventually the infection subsided. But it is still painful.

She told me this five weeks after she had been discharged.

Meg, having her third child, suffered a serious haemorrhage and almost died:

What I was worried about most was the recovery. I knew how weak I was. I knew I couldn't look after the family. That puts a hellish pressure on you. Although there is a follow-up in terms of medical needs – I did have a lot of attention – I really needed someone to come and look after the kids.

Although Meg had lost the fitness and health in her body (for a time), her thoughts about her body were focused on its 'use' in the care of others. Most women recover physically reasonably quickly after the birth. However, what they do lose is, somehow, the autonomy or control over their bodies. It is there for *another* at this stage of their lives.

Breastfeeding

Breastfeeding is a good example of this. You are told that breastfeeding is best for the baby and for yourselves. It is not that clear-cut though and the dilemmas are never fully explained. Jane and Melanie, for example, had both wanted to breastfeed and found they were unable to. The benefits for them turned out to be longer periods of sleep at an early stage, because their babies were not so hungry as a breastfed baby would probably have been.

Norma had found herself constantly feeding a crying hungry baby. It sometimes seemed as if the message that breastfeeding is beneficial was a myth.

If it can be sustained and is not too stressful, breast-feeding helps the mother lose the fat laid down during the pregnancy and thus return to near her normal shape. But breastfeeding can be distressing not just because it can feel like hard work and make your nipples sore. Some women had special difficulties dealing with breastfeeding.

Francis had been alerted, after the birth of her first child, that her nipples were inverted, which made it difficult for the baby to suck. She had to use plastic teats over her nipples which made breastfeeding a difficult and endless process for her:

> *I've worked out a method of feeding which has made all the difference. I've got the milk, but not the nipples. In fact, the milk comes in extremely fast. When she does latch on – it comes out too fast.*

Breastfeeding can intensify the feeling that your body is not your own. Your breasts, once private, are now the property of a demanding other. They are not for you – they produce milk for the baby. Francis called it 'you get cow-like', although she saw it as a challenge declaring that 'I'm jolly well going to do it for four months!' When her baby was six months old, she wrote to me:

> *Yes, I have had moments of depression, especially the first three months when I was breastfeeding and recovering physically.*

Some argue that the physical experience of breastfeeding is a sensual, pleasurable sensation. Most women I spoke to wanted to breastfeed 'for the sake of the baby', but the sensations they experienced were painful.

Ruth experienced engorgement in her breasts:

I had a lot of problems with the feeding. I was engorged and we had to pump it off ... and hot flannels before feeding, cold flannels after. On the third night, around 3 a.m., I was sitting holding the breastpump, my stepmother was pumping it, Roy was pacing up and down with her (the baby). She was screaming her head off. It took three of us one and a half hours for each feed, and this happened three times during the night!

Later that week, I was so engorged, I couldn't put a bra on. I just sat there and dripped and waited until I could take some more off. I was eating all the time. It was a lot tougher than I thought it would be.

Shortly after that, her breasts became infected. But the problem soon cleared up as she had sought medical help straight away.

Sarah told me that breastfeeding had been really painful for her:

It's been so sore, and now it's six weeks on, and I feel it should be getting better. It was the one thing I really wanted – it went really well at first and at three weeks it got sorer. I got really despondent. I think I'm ever so sensitive skin-wise. It hasn't cracked, but I had a couple of days of it getting better and then yesterday I got shooting pains down my arms. Sometimes I have to clench my fists even to think about feeding ... the nice thing though is that he's putting on loads of weight.

The pain does not only happen when trying to feed the baby. When the baby cries, Sylvia found:

> *It hurts. It's like a physical pain. Not only because it activates the milk, but because I cannot concentrate on anything if she is crying.*

The postnatal changes also introduce another layer of losses. Samantha expressed an example of this in a letter to me, when her baby was around six months old:

> *When Ellie was five months old, I finished breast-feeding completely and for a week after that I felt down. I felt as if I had lost some of the closeness.*

Wendy felt the same. In her letter she said: 'I felt most strange coming off breastfeeding. I'm torn between wanting to continue and "doing what's best".'

Feeling too fat

Losing your physical autonomy – feeling your body is not your own – can be a serious loss. By the time you come to the stage of feeding the baby, you are a long way down the process that began with the confirmation of pregnancy. Many of the women I spoke to kept one particular thought going – that was, they wanted to make sure they got their figure back once the baby arrived.

Dion, talking to me when she was pregnant, said:

> *I do sort of feel funny. I haven't really bought a lot of maternity clothes – no dresses. So you do feel*

funny, particularly when you see people in their shorts. You wish you could be like that.

Angela had been particularly concerned about this, as she knew she had a tendency to be overweight and she had put a great deal of effort into weight loss prior to becoming pregnant with her first son. However, she did not achieve this and put on even more weight during the second pregnancy and birth. This remained the case until our last meeting, when her baby was six months old. She felt that being on the pill prevented her from losing weight, so they started using condoms instead:

I don't really want to go on a diet yet – I'm not in that frame of mind. I've got to feel really deter-mined and I don't feel that way at the moment. I was worried about my weight.

Samantha was also worried about her weight.

I've still got half a stone to lose.* Most of it's [the weight gained during pregnancy] gone. I'm into my jeans now – but I had to buy a bigger pair! It's the hips. I didn't have any before. Eric used to say I was like a boy. But for some reason my hips won't go back ... I didn't lose weight as quickly as I thought I would. And I was so disappointed when I wasn't back to my normal figure at the six-week check-up. I couldn't understand it.

* This conversation took place three months after the birth.

Losing your looks

Everyone had a degree of concern about their appearance, even if they were not overweight. Isobel at the final interview told me in some detail:

> **Isobel:** *I suppose in some ways I don't feel young any more. Um, I suppose I feel less feminine – more matronly or womanly in some way that's hard to express. I definitely feel different about myself. I know I'm not as young looking. I know I'm not the same shape as I used to be.*
>
> **Paula:** *What do you mean 'young looking'?*
>
> **Isobel:** *I feel I've got a lot older in the face and since having the baby my hair has gone dreadful – you know things like that. Maybe it's just that I'm not getting out and getting as much exercise. I feel really out of condition. Although I'm back to my normal weight, I'm certainly not back to my normal shape. I've lost a lot of muscle and I'm really flabby in its place.*

Losing the body you knew is not easy to accept for most of us. It is part of our identity. Much of what is 'lost' at this stage is recovered. But there will be permanent changes for some people – scars from Caesarean sections, excess weight, changes in body shape that endure.

Losing your 'mind'

Fatigue and stress have a detrimental effect on mental functioning – memory and concentration as well as perceptions of social events. These are also symptoms of depression. The paradox here then is that loss of sleep, time and self-esteem feed into and bring about depressed moods. These, in turn, aggravate the feeling of losing your mind. It becomes a vicious circle. Most people experienced distress when faced with their reduced abilities:

It's silly things like my memory. Remembering people's names. I went back to visit the people in my office and I couldn't remember their names. I felt really embarrassed. That sort of worried me and I thought 'Oh God, am I going mad?'

Samantha was having these problems three months after the baby's birth. She was particularly concerned, as she had worked her way up to the position she had in the company she worked for. Her background militated against success in the white-collar world. She had made it against the odds, and it worried her that she might no longer be the person she valued. She frequently felt preoccupied. Her husband would speak to her and 'I'm in a world of my own'. She said that it was difficult to know whether this was *caused* by having a baby or simply not using her mind in the way she used to do.

Sylvia, who had previously run an antique-dealing business, realised that, by the time her daughter was three months old, her solicitor husband had all the power. This had happened without her really noticing and she found it distressing.

He takes so much responsibility for the money side of things and paperwork. I tend to be terribly lackadaisical. I never know where the hell I am — whereas before I knew exactly how much money I

had ... I let him get on with it so it's my fault for
letting go.

However, she became increasingly concerned with this
issue (his control of the money) during this and the subsequent interview, when she wanted to discuss it over and
over again. It seemed to represent sanity and autonomy
for her. Without power over her finances, Sylvia found
herself distressed every time she had to think about
buying something for the house and the baby:

I've found making decisions really difficult. For
example, this pushchair business. It's been going
on for weeks and weeks. Making up my mind
which one to get. I make a decision but within
five minutes I chicken out of making one. It's
about the fifth time I've done that. It really
bothers me. I have a bad night's sleep because I
have pushchairs running round and round in my
head ... it is driving me to distraction. Giving me
a lot of problems.

Three months later when I visited Sylvia again, she was
still very concerned about money and her autonomy in
relation to it. 'Oh – I took the pushchair back! And the
highchair ... I think it's me. I take ages making up my
mind and then it's faulty.'
    Sylvia was clearly getting herself knotted up over
things about herself that she valued but had lost. As a
keen and successful businesswoman, money and
decisions about what to buy had been the easy part of
her life. She was good at it, and if she did make
decisions that were not profitable her mistakes had been
outweighed by her successes. The problem was that she

remembered this person – the successful woman and found it difficult to reconcile her with the timid, befuddled person she had become. Her anxiety about the distance between the two seemed to expend her energy and the mental exhaustion she experienced fed into her poor self-image – the stranger she had become.

Penelope, in her forties, the oldest first-time mother among the interviewees, also had had the hardest time postnatally. The birth had been particularly traumatic – premature, but following false alarms, a prolonged stay in hospital and the absence of Roger her partner, during their baby's birth. His behaviour, which I discuss in Chapter 6, was so undermining and unsupportive that Penelope was not only alone in her concern and care for the baby, but had to work to stop Roger and his problems totally weighing her down. She tried hard to maintain a front of normality. She was a highly educated and intelligent woman who worked as a lecturer in a further-education college. She had insisted that I come for lunch when I phoned to arrange my visit, when the baby was three months old. When I arrived at her house though, there was no one in. Just as I was writing a note to leave her, she arrived home with Leah – obviously having no recollection that I would be arriving. She was immediately welcoming and polite, and it was clearly important to her to show that she was coping. Every time the baby – whom she had seated in her highchair – moved, Penelope jumped. She told me that she had met a woman at the local National Childbirth Trust postnatal class who had become a friend and from whom she gained much support:

I had been lost – a sense of one's own needs I had lost. Everything had just overwhelmed me and I felt I was totally [deep sigh] submerged by it ... I

*don't feel totally competent now – but I don't feel
as bad as that now ... but my mind does go quite
blurry.*

Francis, also well educated and a professional publisher,
was very subdued on my third visit, when her baby was
three months old. She was rather nervous and jumpy,
particularly when her older son came into the room. She
told me that 'after my son was born I never thought I'd get
my brain back together', but knowing that she had done,
helped her this time. She was doing a little work at home
in preparation for a return to her office and had a nanny to
help her with the children while she was doing this. Now:

*My brain's very woolly. I forget everything and
have to write everything down – quite literally
from room to room. I forget what I've come into
this room for. Hopeless – but where work is
concerned I seem to be at a different level. But
not so with home. It seems to have gone into a
different groove of my brain.*

It was apparent though from talking to Francis that she
was far more anxious over motherhood than she had ever
been about work. She had done well at school and had
managed her career with ease. What concerned her particularly was being a good mother, and she found it difficult to find ways of judging her 'performance' in this
arena. Feedback at work was achieved in several ways –
praise, criticism and commercial success. Francis felt she
received only criticism from her husband, who was from a
large Spanish family where his intelligent mother had
chosen family over career. Francis was plagued by guilt,
and, like many women, only prepared to take on board

failures and mistakes in mothering. I shall discuss this in more detail in Chapter 5.

Losing your mental capacities can make you very anxious and distressed and feel you are losing your mind. For those who do not have a supportive partner and who have a self-critical personality, this can lead to serious depression.

Losing my self

The self (or self-identity) is more than the sum of the parts. The self is the core of our being – the means by which we experience ourselves as unique. It is the means by which we perceive our consciousness. It includes our sense of our body – biological and physical, our abilities, our appearance and the various preferences, choices and relationships we have. The self is the outcome of our personal history and is also the vision we have constructed for our future. It ties us together, and, without a self, we cannot communicate effectively and we cannot make relationships.

The self, among other things, comprises the various *roles* we play and the ways we describe ourselves to others. They might be mother, wife, psychologist, volunteer, happy person, bad-tempered person and so on. The roles are generally more *public* – those are the parts of us that others see – than the core self, but they are run by (if not always controlled by) it. Social psychologists in the mid-20th century, in North America, proposed that the self develops from infancy through taking on roles, and it is through doing that that we establish our place in the world. We learn what it is like to take on a role in a particular way: how people perceive you when you do that and how you, in turn, make sense of other people's perceptions of you. The early ideas behind this theory came from two sources:

1 The idea of the 'looking glass self' which suggests that we develop our self-image and self-esteem from *how we believe* others see us. If we think they like certain characteristics, we will try and develop them and vice versa. This process goes on for ever and thus, as the person changes over time, the images they see reflected in others will change. Thus we continue to develop over the course of our lives, but the most dramatic development occurs in childhood – from that time much of the development is adjustment.

2 The ideas that come from watching children play. Young children in nursery and early school years *pretend to be others* – mothers and fathers, cowboys and Indians, and cops and robbers. Some games allow children to be each other and other people they know. The point is that we naturally seem to discover the social world, our place in it and our vision of ourselves through the eyes of others.

As part of this set of theories there was an important characteristic that each of us has – that is, that we are *reflexive*. The self is not just a means of seeing and experiencing the world. We also hold 'conversations' with our self – we criticise, try to understand and change – through what we tell ourselves about ourselves following self-reflection! We must have all said many times 'I can't believe I did that' or 'why do I feel so depressed when everything is going my way?' Without reflection and the time to 'talk to our self' about our self, it is difficult to keep in touch with the core self. You lose yourself – and from pregnancy onwards for many of us – this process of loss begins to happen. There is a close connection between feeling you are losing *your mind* and losing *your self*.

The stories of all the women I spoke to involved *some* aspect of their self that they lost – not only their physical being or even some of their mental functioning – but some loss of a sense of who they were. This happened in part because a critical means by which we maintain our identity is being mirrored in the relationships with our friends, family and colleagues. When situations change so radically, as they do following childbirth, it is easy to forget.

Melanie, Shirley and Lynn were all in their thirties when they had their first baby and all were established in a career with firm future plans. Melanie, whose husband gave up his work to help with childcare, found it easy to return to work and her career took off – she discovered parts of her self that had been previously dormant. However, she saw the connection between the new ambitious woman and the person who had had a career. Both Shirley and Lynn had political ambitions, and both continued to be clear about that throughout the transition to their motherhood role. They were supported in their ambitions by their partners, friends and family, and were encouraged and helped to attend meetings and write reports during the postnatal period. These three women had qualitatively different experiences from the others I spoke to. Not only did they have a sense of continuity from before pregnancy, but they and their social-support networks ensured that they were able to maintain their expectations. They were aware of the potential losses, and planned ways of minimising them. They still went through tiredness, bodily changes, anxieties like everyone else, but they were kept (as they kept themselves) in tact, somehow. Other women were well supported or had careers but expressed more ambivalence towards their future – they were unclear what the motherhood role would mean to them. Perhaps they had a more romanticised picture than the other three women. Perhaps they wanted motherhood to change their lives – but were unprepared for exactly how this might happen.

Being clear about who you really are

On all four occasions I met with Shirley (who was 35 years old), she described herself as 'relaxed' about the process. Her partner was older than her and had an adult daughter from his earlier marriage. Shirley had a twin sister who had had a baby a few months before she herself decided to have one, which was a factor in her decision-making:

> **Paula:** *What made you decide to have a baby?*
>
> **Shirley:** *Eh ... time factors probably. Time running out – had to make a decision one way or another. I suppose it is really Sally's [twin sister] experience that had some effect in deciding whether we wanted to take the step or not ... all sorts of vague reasons. Nothing very definite.*
>
> **Paula:** *Were you surprised you enjoyed Sally's baby?*
>
> **Shirley:** *Yes, quite surprised. Yes I was actually. But I had been thinking about it before ... We*

obviously had to make a decision – yes or no. I hadn't been keen on the idea ten years pre- viously, but there wasn't any particular reason. Certainly no pressure. Just something I wanted to do before it was too late.

Shirley did not appear to have a romantic view of mother- hood. It seemed to surprise her that there were pleasures to be had from having a baby. She also had managed to sort out her life over the last few years and be the kind of person she wanted to be, and knew what she wanted. Part of this was to be active in politics, and Shirley said she had become a lot more confident in her abilities since she had been elected onto the local council:

That went reasonably well. I had a reasonable standing within the group and that is a bit of a confidence booster. Also you have to go through the whole process of public speaking which I don't find particularly easy. And you deal with other people's problems – you become a professional com- plainer, sort things out, get things organised for other people and to an extent you can relate all that back to your own problems.

A major factor in her life at present was the sense of control. She and her partner had just undergone the dis- tressing experiencing of having to have a termination because the baby had been diagnosed as having Down's syndrome. Again, she was clear she wanted to terminate that pregnancy, and, even though it was upsetting, she was confident in her decision. She also had a clear picture of how she *did not want to be* as a mother:

I've seen friends of mine who primarily see them-
selves as mother figures. There's a university friend
of mine in Birmingham. She's not so much the
college friend I knew but someone who's bringing
up two kids with another one on the way. She is
largely a mother figure and, though she keeps up
with outside interests, that is her primary concern.
I just don't see myself as doing that.

The birth had been carefully organised. She opted for a
'high tech' maternity unit led by obstetricians who frequently induced the birth when the time was due.
Shirley thus went into hospital early in the morning, the
induction process was started at 9 a.m. and by the late
afternoon her daughter had been born. She had had
little uncertainty about when she would go into labour,
and had had a decent night's sleep prior to the birth and
felt in control. Once again, she had taken a very practical
approach to the birth process and had no particular desire
towards any more 'natural' method. Towards the end of
the meeting we had when her daughter was one month
old, she told me she had both joined the local National
Childbirth Trust in the hope of gaining support with
parenting and been elected as vice-chair of a local political
committee. 'I can manage that on a fairly relaxed
schedule.' She also continued other committee work,
and, at the three-month postnatal stage, she told me that
'OK you get tired and that dulls you to some extent – but I
don't feel that disabled by it. I've just kept going (with my
work), obviously at a slower pace.'

At the last interview, when her daughter was six
months old, she was due to return to her job as a
manager in a trade-union organisation (in addition to
her political commitments). She felt very happy to do
this, as she felt she had taken the mothering role with

her baby as far as she could. She was happy for a professional nanny to take over.

> **Paula:** *One last question — if I were to take you back to a year ago — would you say you were any different now from the way you were then?*
>
> **Shirley:** *I'm much more concerned about being settled. It's a new dimension to my life — I feel much more strongly about Kate than I expected to feel ... I'm much more child-centred than I thought I would be, although, having said that, I'm determined to carry on doing more political things. I've been quite happy over this last six months to be child-centred, but I'm beginning to feel irritated and thinking it's about time to get on with things.*

This is different from most of the other women. Shirley's perception of being child-centred was carefully balanced with fulfilling some of her own needs and being very clear about the boundaries. She realised she could not give up the important part of herself which focused around her political ambitions. Her awareness of her needs prevented her losing herself as she became a mother. She knew how far she felt happy in relation to giving things up for motherhood. She therefore had little guilt and ambivalence.

Francis, on the other hand, wrote to me when her baby was nine months old. She too had kept doing some work during her maternity leave and had a nanny to help her. But even though she was back at work when she wrote, she felt that:

Yes, I have had moments of depression especially the first three months with breastfeeding [she had had the difficulties described above in this chapter] and recovering physically. At six months and now the depression is directed more at my apparent inability to divide myself in two and give both my children equal attention ... I feel slightly schizophrenic at times ... I have changed very little – perhaps I feel a little more grown up.

Motherhood, it seems, for Francis meant offering bits of her self to those she cared for. She rebuked herself for failing (in her eyes) to do this. Her view of being grown-up was similar to the image she had had of her mother whom we discussed when we first met. She felt her parents both wanted children and her mother took on a very traditional role. She never complained about anything, even though Francis felt she might have had grounds. Also her younger brother had been very ill as a child and her mother had had to divide her time between looking after her and her brother. From the age of 12 she attended boarding school and she felt she did well there and got a great deal of attention because she succeeded at her school work. She felt that she had to be perfect at mothering. She felt being grown-up was not complaining.

It is the contrast between self-knowledge, self-confidence and the 'ideal' you set yourself that determines how significant the losses, around the time of early motherhood, can be to your mental health.

It is important to have as clear and accurate a picture of yourself as you can before becoming a mother. It is equally important not to set an impossible ideal which you will certainly fail to live up to.

Finding yourself as a mother

Time, the great emotional healer, also witnesses the development and increased independence of the baby, the growth of that baby into a 'person' and a renewed set of relationships within the family. Women become more familiar with their role as mother or mother of more than one child. Their life moves on and they regain aspects of themselves that had been lost. You can reclaim your body and mind, possibly return to work or at least manage to run the home with time to do things that measure up to your own requirements. You can manage a conversation without having to change a nappy or feed a baby and you can also talk about things other than the day-to-day tasks associated with motherhood. There is no doubt that motherhood changes you. However, the issue is how well you manage to integrate this role *and still be yourself.* If you do not achieve this, then it is possible to experience stress and depression for several years – not necessarily at a clinical level, or even all the time.

George Brown and Tirrill Harris[10] carried out a series of studies about women and depression in urban and rural areas. They found that under some circumstances mothers might remain depressed up until their children were well into school age. There is something about being a mother that can be depressing for many women. It is difficult dealing with the various 'guilt trips' that everyone from the mass media, politicians, novelists and health professionals lay at the feet of *women and mothers.* Men and fathers do not seem to be subject to the same pressures. Neither do they appear to be so vulnerable to child-related guilt, as we shall see in Chapter 5. Facing the paradox of being a mother – the losses as well as the gains –

can help you come to terms with exactly how you feel. It prevents that *selflessness* which is so destructive to a person's mental well-being. Unless someone is able to assert their self and know what they want, they will not be able to help their children do the same. This conversation took place three months after the birth.

Being a 'good' mother: the paradox of sacrifice

Introduction

> *The attention that a baby requires and the resulting fatigue are not always to the parents' liking. And in many cases parents do not pass the 'sacrifice test'.*[1]
>
> *I find the contradiction between the real and the conceptual is more extreme here than in any other area of life. I would throw myself in front of a lorry to prevent damage to the silken little toe of my son, yet half a week's housebound entertaining him due to a cold sets me gagging with boredom and fatigue*[2].

Motherhood – declared universally as woman's greatest *achievement* and the means to fulfilling her femininity – is also the potential source of her emotional *destruction*. In the process of psychological development, we learn how we see the world and how others see us. We do a lot of this development through taking on roles as part of childhood games, and, for young girls, playing 'mother' is a frequent source of learning. The evidence as to whether the fact that, in games such as – mothers and fathers, girls usually take on the role of 'mother' is instinctive or natural is in dispute.

It is difficult to separate the psychological impact on a child encouraged by adults to take on socially approved social roles from 'natural' desire. One thing that is clear though is that most girls see themselves as being mothers at some time in their future lives.

The evidence is also clear that, while most women's lives include motherhood, they are not *circumscribed by motherhood alone*. As Hazel Beckett's study of girls' aspirations showed:

> *The question of motherhood versus career seems, for the majority, to have been stably resolved in the direction of combining them. They seem to have made a unanimous and unconflicted choice to experience occupational involvement, marriage and motherhood*[3].

Women have careers, they have responsibilities in their communities. Even if they would choose otherwise, many are persuaded into employment outside the home for financial reasons. Fewer children are born to married couples than ever before – women live with, rather than marry, their male partners, they get divorced, they live as couples with other women in lesbian relationships and they choose to have children on their own. Women who are infertile, or whose partners are, now have opportunities available to assist them in becoming pregnant*.[4]

---

* IVF does not have a very high success rate and is expensive.

Also there is an increase (formally and informally) of surrogacy, whereby one woman who is able to conceive will bear a child for another woman who cannot.

The contemporary family changed dramatically over the course of the second half of the 20th century and one important factor has been the breakdown of the extended family. People have had to move from their roots to seek work, to follow up educational opportunities and find a life for themselves away from their parents, grandparents, aunts and siblings. This means that social support around the time of having a baby can be a problem, particularly when large distances are involved. In the case of some of the women in this study, instead of being able to rely on local support from a few people, one person, often a mother, has had to come and stay for a limited amount of time. This can add further stresses and strains. It is also more than likely that mothers and aunts are in employment and, even if they live nearby, are not as accessible sources of support, however willing, as they might have been to a previous generation.

New mothers therefore are in a difficult position – they have to be superwomen – both self-reliant and an effective 24-hour, 7-days-a-week carer. Contemporary society has failed to take issue with this paradox. Many women, because of this, feel guilty, inadequate and bad mothers, a vision of themselves compounded by a 'secret' guilt surrounding ambivalence towards both their role as mother and their children. This guilt occurs because many of us believe that somehow motherhood is sacred – a mother has to be good and a woman should be a good mother. Motherhood is a major source of depression for many women, particularly in the months after birth when these issues are acute.

What has happened to make women feel bad about themselves as *mothers*, when their behaviour is in most cases more effectively child-focused than that of many fathers? One reason is that it is widely believed that women have a *maternal instinct*.

What is the truth about the maternal instinct?

It is, of course, a matter of debate whether what we call maternal instincts are instincts in the sense of innate patterns of activity[5].

Maternal love is a human feeling. And like any feelings, it is uncertain, fragile and imperfect. Contrary to many assumptions, it is not a deeply rooted given in women's natures'.[6]

The notion of the maternal instinct is now deeply instilled in Western society. The term refers to a widespread and apparently scientifically valid set of beliefs that women have a biological desire to have children, that women have innate capacities to care for children and that women who do not experience this are not truly feminine. The corresponding theories, that reinforce this view, are those proposed by the psychoanalyst John Bowlby[7] during but particularly after World War Two. These ideas came to be known as the 'maternal deprivation thesis'; that is, that an infant who has periods of separation from its mother is likely to suffer severe emotional disturbance in adolescence and adulthood. There are important as-pects to Bowlby's work, such as those discussed in Chapter 4 about the profound emotions associated with loss. However, his early work has been used ideologically and politically to influence beliefs about gender, the family and emotional development, and underpinned popular knowledge about what makes a good mother.

The maternal instinct then refers to the popular idea that women have a *biological compulsion* to become mothers, and that motherhood is a *natural and desirable state for all women*. Indeed, it has been widely argued that it is the pinnacle of femininity and the main focus of a woman's life. Sigmund Freud is famous for arguing this way, suggesting that women who take up careers or other activities are merely sublimating their desire towards motherhood and femininity. He argues that non-maternal women really want to be like men. That, he argued, is against nature and Freud labelled this state 'penis envy'. Unsurprisingly, this view has been widely challenged but the image and underlying belief has not disappeared. Many feminists and other researchers into gender development have argued that it is women's *ability* to carry out a number of roles successfully, including motherhood, that is natural. Men are the one's with the 'lack', because they do not seem to be able to manage the complexity demanded by effectiveness in the public domain of work and the domestic domain as successfully as women.

Is maternal instinct a biological drive?

The idea of the existence of a maternal instinct was posed by childcare experts in the early 19th century and has continued to capture popular imagination despite criticism, particularly from feminist researchers and scholars. The concept of the maternal instinct leaves little room for individual differences in the feelings and behaviour of women who become mothers. The existence of a maternal instinct assumes that *all* women have a biological drive towards conceiving and bearing children. This means that it would therefore be 'unnatural' for a woman not to feel this drive. The women I spoke to, however, did not fit into this pattern. Some had a strong desire to have a child but had not always felt that way. Penelope, who did have a biological explanation for her desire for a child, did not feel strongly until she reached the age of 40 with a good career behind her. Then she said:

> *I suppose it's a fulfilment. A personal fulfilment different from other aspects of fulfilment. It's a very strong biological urge – I can't explain it in any other way. I just wanted to have a baby – for a lot of emotional reasons. I knew time was running out. But [sigh] I also suspect it was about the need for stability and ummm ... I've always been a late developer. I suppose inevitably having a baby later made sense in terms of my whole life.*

Wendy also felt that she had wanted a baby for as long as she could remember. However, it was not an urgent need:

> *We have been planning a pregnancy for some time. But it had been put off and put off and then I had a coil fitted, which was due to come out after three years. But when I went for a check-up they couldn't find it, so I had to have an operation to take it out some weeks later.*

She then conceived by accident. Although she was delighted to be pregnant, Wendy had just had a promotion at work and said proudly that next time I visited (that was to be when the baby was about a month old), she hoped to be getting settled in her new post – clearly her priority at that stage. But did she feel the drive to motherhood?

> **Paula:** *If I had told you 20 years ago that you couldn't have children – how do you think you would have felt?*
>
> **Wendy:** *I'd probably thought about adopting.*
>
> **Paula:** *So you definitely saw motherhood as part of your future?*
>
> **Wendy:** *Yes, but I can remember recently thinking 'if I can't have one – I shan't let it ruin my life. It won't get me old and bitter'. Like if I miscarry – it happens and I will take things as they come.*

So, although Wendy clearly wanted her baby, there were other things that made up her life.

Jerri had given the matter of motherhood very little thought until she became pregnant:

> *I never ever felt maternal – ever in my life never. Not that I disliked babies, but certainly I've never been that attracted to them. It took a lot of thinking about – this 30 thing – everyone said what are you going to do about it.*
>
> *When I found out I was pregnant I felt wonderful and felt very maternal – and I actually gave it a lot of thought and consideration. I didn't do it because it was the norm.*

Once the possibility of a baby became a reality, her perception towards having maternal feelings changed dramatically. This is common with many women – the fact of pregnancy or the arrival of a baby makes a great deal of difference emotionally. It changes your view of motherhood, and the image of yourself as a mother begins to take shape. But how far is this a biological drive? What women themselves appear to be saying does not fit in particularly well with the notion of a maternal instinct. Most take a more practical view of the process of wanting to become a mother. Isobel was particularly practical in her planning:

Paula: *What made you want to get pregnant at this stage?*

Isobel: *It came into the long-term plans. Until now we were getting this place (their flat) in order and I didn't want to leave it too long. It had been planned. And it happened as we planned it!*

Paula: *So you're pleased about that?*

Isobel: *Oh yes, yes.*

Paula: *Is being a mother something that has always been important to you?*

Isobel: *I don't know. I suppose I always wanted to have children – but I don't lean over prams and say nice things to them. But, at the same time, I'm quite easy with children.*

Is there a paternal instinct?

In several instances, the people I talked to had not particularly seen motherhood as *their* decision. They had been happy enough but there was no major imperative, and it was their partner who had the drive.

Sylvia, who had been a keen and successful business-woman, thought when she got married that motherhood was a reasonable future possibility:

Paula: *What made you want to have a baby now?*

Sylvia: *Well, my husband thinks he is ancient – he's 34! All his friends are well stuck into the baby stage – so he's very keen. Oh – I'm keen as well. No specific reason … I've never really given it much positive thought. It's always been that in the future one does get married and has a family – and then suddenly it's a reality!*

Is biology destiny?

The theory of the maternal instinct suggests that the drive *to give birth* leads naturally and explicitly towards the need to *raise* a child. The fact of having a womb, ovaries and breasts, and the potential to conceive, leads naturally and indisputably to wanting to look after the baby and child. The proponents of this belief take a firm view that biology is destiny and biological femininity is a template for being a naturally good mother – the opposite of which is true for men.

It is clear that women and men give different meanings to their bodies and have different experiences of socialisation. But it is very difficult to disentangle what women do *because they are born female*, and what they do because of complicated *cultural processes* that intervene between the biological body and the mind in the course of their upbringing.

In practice, then, taking the view that biology is destiny means not only the desire to fulfil the emotional and practical needs of the child, but it also means taking the negative aspects of the *lifestyle* that Joanna Briscoe[2] describes in the quotation above. Is it 'natural' for a mother to *desire* to take full responsibility for spending most of *her* time with her child? What then can we say about the frustration, boredom and feelings of personal inadequacy that are bound to emerge when an intelligent, lively adult focuses almost exclusively on others' needs. This is a major self-sacrifice that is likely to result in a severe depression if the woman seriously believes that this *is* her destiny.

But being a 'good' mother and self-sacrifice do not conform with most women's accounts of their needs and would not *seem* to be natural, just or in the best interests of the child. It does not even seem to be in the best interests of men or other family members to use these simplistic biological arguments to ensure that childcare responsibilities reside with the mother. Survival – both physical and emotional – are most commonly based on a compromise. But compromise, in a social context where there are expectations that mothers should take on board most of the mundane childcare tasks, frequently leaves women feeling guilty and having to justify themselves.

Adrienne, whose financial circumstances were lavish by the standards of the others I spoke to, did have a choice. She had a three-year-old son and talked to me while she was expecting her second baby. She had had both a maternity nurse for a few months after his birth and a nanny (or several nannies as it turned out) ever since. She also had weekend help when the nanny was not there:

> *My parents decided I should have a nanny. Myself – I can't see how anyone can cope day in day out even if they **adore** children. Without a break they would have to be extremely healthy. I was alone for three weeks with him, living with my in-laws. When he yelled – there I was ... Anyone who doesn't have a nanny has to take them absolutely everywhere.*

Adrienne then is arguing that motherhood is hard work and women need a break. She is also questioning the value to women of being in the constant company of their children. Even to Adrienne, who believes that women's first commitment should be to their husband and children, this does not imply the denial of a self and selfish needs.

Were you born knowing how to bath a baby?

Another aspect of the maternal instinct theory is that the skills and capacities for caring for infants and children emerge naturally as part of being a *woman who has become a mother*.

Hilary, a competent and confident professional, nevertheless became very stressed and anxious about her ability to do 'maternal' things and got 'desperate' sometimes when she attended clinics with her first daughter:

*I always managed to get her jumper stuck on her
head or something – and thought all other mothers
were watching – and all I was trying to do was get
her undressed so she could be weighed. I would be
seething with fear – anxiety the whole time. I don't
think I'll do that again – I hope I don't. [Laugh].
Also bathing I think is the occasion when you think
they're the most vulnerable and you're the most
cack-handed.*

*I used to get upset about really silly things –
and what was odd was when he [her husband]
would say 'what have you done?' It didn't seem
much – but it was difficult to convey just what it
took out of you really. And then I tried to compare
it with how I felt at work. Did I used to feel this
tired? Was there actually **this** sort of pressure?
And, although it was a really pressurized job, I
don't think it was as hard as the fist few – or just
the first three months.*

It is no coincidence perhaps that many fathers declare
themselves to be 'better' with older children than they
are with babies. As Charlie Lewis[8] has shown in his
study of fatherhood, men are not particularly enthusiastic
about infant care or the *routine* childcare tasks. But they
do come into their own when reading children bedtime
stories, taking them to the park, playing games and (sometimes) giving them baths.

The father's role

Gwen found her husband's apparent lack of emotional
connection with the baby exasperating. She believed she

had the skills to care for the baby because she had learned them. Furthermore, she demonstrates contradiction and unconscious conflict in her account of her husband's role as father and hers as a mother:

Paula: *Is she equally central to both of you?*

Gwen: *Yes, definitely.*

Paula: *That must be a support to you. How does his interest manifest itself?*

Gwen: *When he comes home in the evening he'll want to take over and give me a rest. If I want to go out he's more than happy to look after her, change nappies and all the rest of it. And she does take bottles, so if I want a rest I'll go and make a bottle and he'll do it. I was just exhausted yesterday. I felt totally drained by the time i got up in the morning and I wanted to go back to bed. But there were things to do and people to see so I couldn't really.*

Paula: *So going back to your husband. There's no complaint on your side that he's leaving you to cope alone?*

Gwen: *Well, sometimes ... general little niggles. Um, if he comes in and I suppose he's got so used to me breastfeeding that it doesn't occur to him to say 'would you like a rest?' I have to* **ask** *and having had a hard day at the office, he'll come home and switch the box on and just sit. And if he's holding her he'll just sit her on his lap. Not really talk to her or anything. And* *if I'm downstairs I can hear her whingeing and crying. It sets me on edge. I'll storm back upstairs and say 'She's a little human being you know, she does get bored. Talk to her!' But apart from that he is beginning to learn that he has to show her things ... to hold her attention or else she'll start crying again. I think it's easier for us to learn. For the men, it's tremendously difficult ... I'm here all day. He doesn't think about it.*

It is clear that Gwen believes that parent skills are learned from spending time with the baby and that they are learned because a parent puts effort into doing so. The way she changed her description of her husband's behaviour, as I questioned her more closely, indicated that it made her angry and possibly embarrassed that he seemed so lacking in empathy both with her and the baby. She did not hold a belief that baby care was either 'natural' to her or that it was her responsibility alone.

Is a good woman the same as a good mother?

Most women want to be seen as feminine and womanly, whatever their choice of lifestyle. However, the theory of the maternal instinct makes it clear that a woman who does not have the skills and capacities and desires that characterise the maternal woman is not truly feminine. She is the object of pity or derision.

Very recently, this view of femininity and the social role of women has been stridently supported in the mass media by a sociobiological or evolutionary psychology approach to understanding relationships between men and women. This approach to human nature proposes that not only have we evolved *physically* over millions of years, but *our minds have evolved as well.* Because it is believed that a major human impetus is to ensure that our genes are passed on to a subsequent generation, women and men have different approaches to 'mating'. Women take nine months to have each child and thus they are seen to have 'greater investment' in each one. This has led them to develop characteristics that make them choosy about their choice of mate – they want the father of their child to have the best genes that they are able to attract. Men, who can technically father several babies in the course of a day, 'mate' with as many women as they can. Thus it is the men who can persuade women to have sex with them who are successful in this context. To be so, they have to be aggressive, assertive and not spend too much time on each offspring. They are most likely to achieve their reproductive aim if they move on. Women, on the other hand, are successful if they rear these relatively few children into adulthood so they in turn may reproduce. This, over millions of years, has led to development of the general characteristics of each sex, it is argued. Women have evolved to be sexually choosy and to put maximum effort into rearing each child. As one well-known sociobiologist summarised the argument:

> *Men and women have different bodies. The differences are the direct result of evolution. Women's bodies evolved to suit the demands of bearing and rearing children ... Men and women have different minds. The differences are the direct result of evolution. Women's minds evolved to suit the*

demands of bearing and rearing children and of gathering plant food.[9]

This approach provides a logical, biologically driven explanation of why women should be at home with the children and why men (hunters) should be out of the home providing for the family. This view is very appealing, particularly to those who wish to maintain the status quo. But why then, if women are adapted to being in the home and rearing children, do so many human females find the stay-at-home mothering role frustrating and/or depressing? Why do women like Melanie (who has taken the provider/hunter role), Lynn and Shirley (who have had, and continue to be true to, their long-term career plans) be both proud and happy to be mothers, and also content with them*selves*?

Hilary articulated the case very well:

I do think most women I know have been much better in their jobs then the men I know. I don't think – perhaps that's unfair to men – but it's been my experience over a long period of time really. That's what I felt about me in the past. I was better than men I know. Maybe I'd made a big thing about that in the past. Maybe I felt that I'd got confidence despite being a woman in a man's world. And being forced back into the woman's role and actually finding it so stressful – exaggerated it – I think that was true. All of a sudden, you're forced to being back with women. Having been out and feeling equal, free and confident – all of a sudden, I was pushed back into a woman's position. I didn't like it – I just couldn't cope. It didn't feel good – and part of me didn't want it to feel good. 'I don't want to be an expert at changing nappies!'

Despite this clear understanding of herself and the context in which she managed her life, she sacrificed much of her self following the birth of her second child 18 months after her first, because being a *good* mother was very important to her.

But, what does make a good mother?

Belief in the all powerful mother spawns a recurrent tendency to blame the mother on the one hand, and a fantasy of maternal perfectibility on the other.[10]

The question of what makes a good mother is also paradoxical. We are constantly confronted by experts in child-rearing in the mass media, in child health clinics, nurseries and in books. They proclaim that children *need* their mothers (usually) with them most of the time to provide love and intellectual stimulation. These are also the proclamations of many contemporary developmental psychologists. It is also argued now that depressed mothers can damage the emotional and intellectual development of their infant or child. A depressed mother is not 'there' for her child and a depressed mother might lead to a depressed child. However, there is an important contradiction in the way that these views are put across to the public. While children suffer from being with a depressed mother, there is little attention paid to the needs of that mother. The overriding suggestion is that such women *seek medical help* in order to provide what their child needs from them. In other words, the woman is seen as suffering from an illness that can be treated, usually with antidepressants. Little if any thought is given to the *mother's* quality of life. What a dilemma – and what a responsibility!

The business about what kind of mother to be can be very confusing. Norma, for example, was caught in the dilemma of not wanting to be a mother like hers had been, although she appreciated the commitment her mother had made to her care. Norma also recognised her mother's sacrifice and 'obliteration' as a person in her own right:

Norma: *I kind of thought that if I have a baby, that's the end of me as a person. I'd never be able to do anything again, but then one of my sisters is a single mother and she's gone on to university. And she was very supportive ... and said there's life afterwards! I think that helped a lot.*

Paula: *What made you think that way?*

Norma: *Well, I don't know. I don't have many friends who have babies. The women I work with have babies. I just look after women and babies for seven days and then they go back into the community*. But you see women on buses with pushchairs – and I think of my own experience of my own mother. She was a midwife and gave up work to have children and her whole life revolved around us. I felt that – it's a very Irish thing, I suppose – but*

---

* Norma is a midwife.

to be a good mother I'd have to be at home all the time to really give myself. And I just liked to have my freedom, and as I say most of my friends are very independent. And I thought ... well, they won't want to know me. My friends won't want to be around me and a crying baby. You go to a party and there's a woman with a baby. In a way she is excluded. She ends up running after the baby − feeding, changing it. It's different, you know. I was very frightened. I thought this is it. I'm just going to come to a stop and I didn't think I'd be able to organise myself enough to do all the things I wanted to do.

Sarah Clement,[11] a psychologist who is now an expert on reproductive health herself, wrote in some detail about her experiences of becoming a mother and the choices she made. She was two years into doing her PhD (in her mid-twenties) when she became pregnant, having wanted a child for a long time. 'Mad as this may sound it was a planned event. I had visions of myself tapping away at my word processor to the coos of a sleeping baby, attending seminars with a baby snuggled in a sling, of a toddler happily playing in a playpen while I studied.

Sarah started working on the PhD again when her son was about a month old, and, with good sense, concentrated on transcribing tapes and other mechanical tasks. '... although I'm somewhat dubious of the view that fluctuating hormones after childbirth mess up your mind, memory and concentration, lack and disruption of sleep do tend to have this effect.' She had to do all her work while her son slept during the day − but she found that, although he slept for many hours, they weren't always regular or predictable. She herself had to take some daytime sleep as well, to catch up with what she had missed in the night. Furthermore:

> *There are so many other things to do in that precious time when the baby is asleep. Like having some time to yourself, say, to have a bath or relax, having time for your relationship with your partner, time to cook and eat and time to sleep.*

Sarah also came up against the anti-baby society – the difficulties of taking pushchairs around the shops or on public transport, the places where babies are unwelcome and the disapproval of others for discreet breastfeeding in public places. When her baby was six months, she found she had to opt for part-time childcare. This, of course, is an alternative only open to those with enough money and only applies to the average student if they have the financial backing of a partner or parent. For Sarah though, despite the drawback of combining career or study and early motherhood, she found the experience overwhelmingly worth it. Despite the clear and longstanding desire she had had to have a baby, she admitted that full-time motherhood without the balance with intellectual achievement would have been very difficult for her. Her experience also enabled her to focus and appreciate time with the baby and time for pursuing her own goals.

It is possible for a woman to reconcile her desire to be a mother, her love for her child and the sacrifice of her own needs with the wish to maintain a sense of self-hood. It is an extraordinary paradox that mothers have to face: Myself or my baby? The traditional retort is 'the baby comes first.' But what about maternal depression? How can you give anything of value to the baby if you cannot care for yourself?

Negotiating the boundaries between self and other

Most of the psychological studies of gender and of motherhood show that caring for one's self is difficult for many women. It is also hard for women to put forward, or take seriously, the kinds of *idea* intended to liberate women from this way of behaving and thinking. Terri Apter,[12] writing about whether feminism has changed women's attitudes to being mothers, found:

> *Here was a popular movement telling women to be firm, to be fierce to be independent and even to be selfish, to turn their backs on the men they were used to looking for support – a movement which opened up such truths that it seemed to release many women from a prison. Yet because the women who embraced the tenets of feminism had grown up amid the stereotype of a dependent, compliant woman, they experienced considerable anxiety when faced with the realisation of feminist goals.*

Shaking off the need to relate to others in a *selfless* way is a problem. Women frequently find they are putting others first, or behave dependently towards them. Women typically listen to their friends' problems for hours, but find it difficult to get anyone to listen to them. Women feel they should be the ones to take responsibility (particularly) for heterosexual relationships. Women certainly feel it is their responsibility to make the arrangements for childcare and domestic chores, even if that means organising someone else to do it. Why do women feel like this?

Theories of gender and popular beliefs about women, in particular, identify femininity as being *relational* (i.e women, by nature and by socialisation, make *connections* with others). Their interests, behaviours, speech styles and emotions converge around a vision of femininity in which women focus upon others and themselves in relation to others. The well-known psychotherapist Susie Orbach, writing with her colleague from the Women's Therapy Centre, Louise Eichenbaum, make clear:

> *The first psychological demand that flows from a woman's social role is that she must **defer** to others, follow their lead, articulate her needs only in relation to theirs. In essence, she is not to be the main actor in her own life. As a result of this social requirement, women come to believe they are not important in themselves for themselves. Women come to feel they are unworthy, undeserving and unentitled. Women are frequently self-deprecating and hesitant about their own initiatives. They feel reluctant to speak for themselves, to voice their own thoughts and ideas, to act on their own behalf. Being pushed to defer to others means that they come to undervalue and feel insecure about themselves, their wants and their opinions. A recognition of a woman's own needs can therefore be complicated and a process occurs in which women come to hide their desires from themselves.*[13]

Women reading this first time around might disagree strongly with their thesis. The language of the experts in this extract presents a most unforgiving perspective on girls' and women's experiences and their desires and ability to change them. But a second and closer reading rings true to many women's stories about the transition to motherhood and the postnatal weeks and months. To willingly become a mother means that (at least, for a significant amount of time) the responsibility of care involves putting others before yourself. You may be a solicitor, housewife, social worker or scientist but it is difficult to avoid the responsibilities of motherhood. The pressure may appear to come from outside – a hard-working partner who has no spare time for childcare, for example. But, ultimately, it is the mother herself who is caught in the dilemma. Who am I? Whose needs are paramount? The answer is usually – the children. The guilt we feel when trying to assert ourselves against the needs of a vulnerable baby often means a sense of self-loathing or disgust. How dare I want to go out with my friends, go to work, have a career, have time with my partner or whatever the competing, self-pleasuring demand. It is the needs of the baby and then the partner that win out. If they don't, we suffer in other ways. Whatever we choose– the path of self-interest and guilt or self-sacrifice and resentment – we feel inadequate as a mother. Even women who are described as 'perfect' in their maternal role know the truth – that there are many times when they wish they were elsewhere.

Understanding the implications of what Eichenbaum and Orbach have to say might be the start of managing our emotional *boundaries*, so we can preserve our 'self' and give to others in a way that benefits everyone and encourages emotional development. Many women's experience of growing up as a girl and woman, in a society that is essentially run and organised by men, is that recognising the boundaries between yourself and the others who want you to care for them becomes a difficult task. This is because many women have not practised identifying their own needs and learning to distinguish them from the needs of others.

Satisfying your own needs is not equivalent to behaving like a strident harridan. It can be a very gentle process and include the desire to be a good and caring mother.

Sarah Clement's experience discussed above was one example. Ruth, whom I interviewed, was another. When I visited Ruth the third time, when her daughter was three months old, she had managed to take control of some of her important needs – inparticular, the need for a social life and friends of her own. She had had a very stressful job as a lecturer to professional health carers in a further-education college, and, despite her awareness that she would at some point need to return to a career, she was still experiencing relief from the stress of her job. She felt she had slowed down and her stepmother had told her: 'you're not chasing your tail like you used to before.' Her life had been 'work, travelling and fitting in a social life.' Now she was able to give time and consideration to what she wanted and needed at any particular time:

> *If I've felt tired I've just gone to bed in the afternoon and not done much. I've got the opportunity to do that. Whereas I feel that if you do try to push yourself, it makes you feel so much worse.*

It was summer at the time of this interview and she and her husband both enjoyed that time of year. Their focus was upon the *social* and they had a pub they would go to after he came home from work two or three times a week. The weather had been good and they could sit out in the pub garden. 'We'll just go and chat over a drink.' A few weeks beforehand, when I had done the previous interview, one of the things that had bothered Ruth had been the lack of opportunity for her husband and herself to talk. They could now make time for this.

She was managing to enjoy motherhood itself now. Her daughter was becoming more responsive in contrast to a few weeks previously, when 'all my time was spent on feeding and changing – I still spend the same amount of time on her – but it's a bit more pleasurable time.'

Ruth had made friends at a postnatal support group, and she went out in the evenings with some of these women without their babies as well as meeting during the day. Even so, 'I haven't met anyone who I feel is "my person" really. They're very pleasant, but what we have in common is the children.'

This led her to recognise that being at home with her new daughter was a *phase* in her life. She was not doing all the things that she herself would choose to do, but, as in the very early days, she had been well supported, and she also had made a decision to leave her stressful job as a result of the pregnancy. She felt very positive towards being a mother at home.

She considered that 'I'm sure it gets monotonous as time goes by.' Ruth therefore was not trapped in a situation that was out of her control. She had managed to alter the pace of her life to fit in with her role. She was able to make relationships on a superficial and pragmatic basis and appreciate the value of them. Her mothering at this stage enabled her to get a reasonable amount of time and pleasure to meet some of her needs. She had set the boundaries to what she identified as her self at that time (i.e. a new mother). She recognised her needs in that context and maintained those boundaries. This did not mean that she avoided unexpected pressure or was totally inflexible in what she chose to do.

Voices of the experts

It may be hard to believe, in the face of the enthusiastic proclamations of contemporary childcare experts, but child-rearing and beliefs about what is best for the growing child are dictates of fashion and culture. The work of the French historian, Elisabeth Badinter,[1] on the history of motherhood, shows how infant care in particular could be quite brutal and, in many cases, infanticide was practised as a means of controlling family size. Women from the middle classes would probably have wet-nurses for their babies – this wet nurse would be a lactating woman from a lower social class who would care for the middle-class woman's baby along with her own in her own home. The less well off would send their new baby to a 'farm' to care for their infants in the early weeks, while upper-class women would have their own live-in nursemaids. All of these practices would have been perfectly normal and acceptable, in some cases as recently as 90 to 100 years ago.

Denise Riley[14] chronicled the growth of 'professional' childcare expertise, which appears to have responded more closely to *economic* than to psychological or emotional imperatives. The needs of the labour market had a greater impact on the popularised views about what is best for the child than any science. The best and most frequently quoted examples are those following the demobilisation of the military after World War Two. Women had been encouraged to hold a variety of occupations normally held by men during the war – from the clerical to heavy manual. Nurseries were opened (often in the workplace) and publicity campaigns encouraged women to take these jobs. The spectre of men returning from the war, without jobs to go to, brought about not only the closure of the nurseries but a sustained campaign to encourage women to stay at home with their children. There was suddenly publicity given to the claims of child care experts, such as John Bowlby,[7] about emotional damage caused by maternal deprivation. There was also a campaign to encourage couples to have more children in the aftermath of the war.

More recently, there has been an initiative by the British government* to get mothers, particularly single mothers, off state benefits. Mass-media campaigns have highlighted comments from senior ministers that mothers can best support their children by having a wider experience of the world of work – thus they can impart more knowledge to the next generation (presumably than the mothers who spent the first few years of their child's life with them at home to prevent them experiencing maternal deprivation)!

The perfect mother (or parent) is a variable concept then, but one that pervades the social fabric and is therefore unavoidable. The voices of the experts are not only used for propaganda purposes but they also shore up the mechanisms of the state that take a 'policing' role towards mothers and fathers. The social and health-care services take on responsibility for the assessment of good and bad ways to be parents. In some cases, where child abuse and sexual abuse occur in families and childcare institutions, there are easily acceptable divides between good and bad.

However, there have been recent cases in the UK and USA, which demonstrate just how spurious the notion of 'good' actually is and just how much it changes with the fashion and imperatives of the mass media. The cases involve the 'Internet adoption' couple and the IVF

* During the administration of New Labour from 1997 to 2001.

treatment provided for a 56-year-old woman. The first case involved a British couple (who already had children) 'buying' twins in the USA and arranging adoption in Arkansas, where the laws were relatively lax. What informs the notion of what makes a good mother is that the couple who adopted the children had a great deal of media exposure which highlighted flaws, particularly in the woman. These resulted in the twins being taken into care. The case is likely to continue, but the media comments have been particularly enlightening. Joanna Moorhead in the *Guardian*[15] outlines the 'charge' of substandard parenting laid against the couple: dirty house, pictures of the woman drinking alcohol in a hotel bar until 2 a.m., acres of television footage of the couple being angry about what had happened to them, the woman's belief in ghosts, her apparent inability to cradle a baby's head properly and her tendency to histrionics. The man was accused of working long hours and not seeing his children. The implication of drawing attention to this is that, while the British nation berated this couple, the idea might slowly dawn that none of us is perfect in this respect.

The second case is that of a couple[16] – the woman 56 years of age and the man 55 – who had had IVF treatment to enable her to conceive, and, at the time the story broke, she was pregnant with twins. The criticism was that, at her age as a mother, she would have no energy to cope and that, at crucial stages of the children's lives, they will be far older than other children's parents. Gynaecologists and experts on IVF, who were interviewed in support of this article, made it clear that they made subjective judgements as to whether or not to treat a couple; that is, that doctors decided who would make a good parent. In this case, one side argued that they only offered treatment to younger women and the other that it was on the basis of suitability of the family circumstances. Adoption experts argued that the needs of the child should be paramount. The point of all this for me is that being a good mother is a matter of fashion and subjective judgement. Most of us manage to avoid the judgement of the social care and health agencies. Even so, we are judged by our partners, our parents, friends, ourselves and in the end by our children. The well-known and often-quoted Donald Winnicott,[17] for all his pronouncements upon the role of woman as mother which supported the maternal deprivation thesis, asserted that, on the whole, it is 'good enough' mothering that enables a child to develop into an emotionally healthy adult. It seems that being good enough is the only goal that makes sense for our mental and physical well-being.

Postnatal depression by proxy

Introduction

A major concern of many postnatally depressed women is guilt at the burden their illness places on their spouses, even as they feel cut off from them and their family.[1]

The views of some experts on PND, although intended to confirm women's distressing postnatal experiences, lay blame and responsibility for the depression on the woman herself. Suggesting that a woman's distress places a burden on her partner does not really help us understand the problem or reach a solution. In fact, this approach leads us round in a vicious circle. The woman has the physical burden and (usually) the immediate and majority of the childcare burden. Women who find the strain of this particularly severe are those who lack support. Support from the partner is not only about 'helping' with some of the domestic tasks. Support is about sharing those tasks equally because both partners have become parents.

There seems to be little acceptance of this perspective on parenthood among most experts. It is seen as a feminist point of view and thus treated as extreme. In most of the self-help books and academic studies, it is the women who become depressed who are treated as the 'problem'. They are portrayed as ill and viewed directly as in need of cure. This is very different from the view taken by the women I talked to.

The notion of who is responsible for PND suggests yet another paradox. Are women victims or culprits? Are mothers to blame if they become depressed postnatally? Do we know for sure that women feel guilty because they are depressed? Who is responsible for their partner's distress if the mother becomes a 'burden'?

All 'sick' or injured people probably have guilt feelings if they are receiving high levels of care and, especially, if they themselves are being 'awkward' and unrewarding as patients or partners, as many in that situation are perceived to be.

PND is far more complex than simply another 'illness'. It occurs in a very specific context with one person, the mother, faced with physical and psychological work to do to ensure the smooth transition of the infant into childhood. The PND-as-illness approach to the problem fails to help us appreciate what triggers PND or to discover remedial actions. However, we do know that a new mother is far less likely to become, or stay, depressed if she has good social support, particularly from the baby's father. But, with the arrival of a new baby, whether it is the first or not, there will be a major shift in the dynamics and relationships within the family. The physical and psycho-social factors, that might bring about depression in the woman, might have a similar effect on the father (and possibly the other children) (Figure 3).

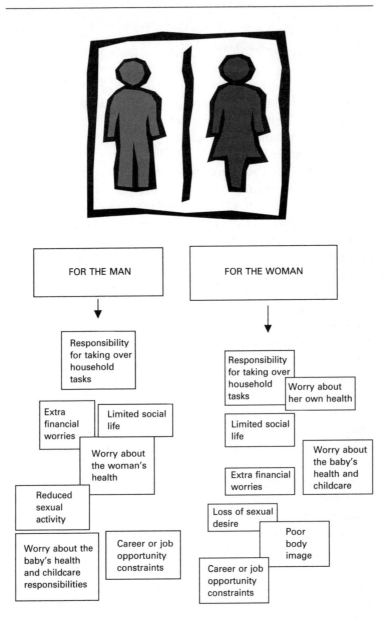

Figure 3   The burden of care.

The paradoxical burden

A study by Elizabeth Boath[2] and her colleagues at Keele University in the UK highlighted the fact that when a woman becomes depressed following childbirth, a clearly identified burden is placed upon other members of her family. Wider implications of the experience of living with and caring about a depressed mother have not been discussed fully by experts or even lay groups. There is, however, a long tradition in social science at looking at the transition to parenthood for both women and men, and the impact that being parents has upon each of them individually and on their relationships. Studies which take a perspective over time, following the transition to parenthood, show that becoming parents reduces intimacy between a couple – they have less time to talk, to share a social and sexual life. Other studies have indicated that pregnancy and the postnatal period may have a negative impact on sexual desire in women, which may, if not discussed in a mutually supportive way, lead to problems in (hetero)sexual relationships. Sexual desire for the woman may be further reduced following a badly repaired episiotomy. Pain and distress during intercourse, as a consequence, may last for as long as a year, causing distress to both partners. Pregnancy and the postnatal period have been shown to coincide with the onset or increase in domestic violence, and it has been suggested recently that many health-care professionals mistake the signs of being a victim of domestic for postnatal depression. There is also evidence that the introduction of a new baby into a family may bring about not only envy from the older child or children, but may result in the older child being physically abusive towards the baby. The transition to parenthood might lead a family to become closer or it might lead to deep rifts, because of disagreements over what is best for the new baby.

The paradox here is this. It is the woman who needs full support to maintain her self, and all that that entails, during the weeks and months after a baby is born. Good-quality social support is overwhelmingly the most important factor involved in either preventing PND or alleviating symptoms and reducing the risk of severe and prolonged depression. The baby also needs time and attention from those who support the mother. However, the partner, other children, grandparents and friends who offer support might also experience the negative aspects of the arrival of the infant in their own right. This might well be described as PND by proxy. Disturbed nights, extra domestic responsibilities, anxiety, and losses such as relationships, economic security, the opportunity to succeed by taking the initiative at work, leisure time and activities, time with friends and so on, are all likely to be part of the new father's experience. Many men find it difficult to cope. They do not expect things to change a great deal for them, and it is difficult for many men to explain to friends that they can no longer do the social things they used to do because they have to take an active parenting role (Figure 4).

It can be a vicious circle. Boath's evidence indicates that this problem is more widespread than the coverage by experts has previously indicated.

The prevailing rhetoric of writers in the area of PND, such as Katherina Dalton, has been focused upon the woman returning to the 'person she used to be' for the sake of her husband.* The woman is 'ill', her body and mind are to blame for the disruption. Her partner is also

---

* Husband is the term Dalton uses most to describe the father of the baby.

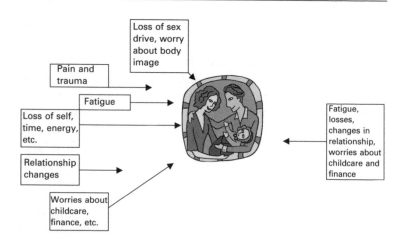

Figure 4   The impact of the baby on the father: postnatal
depression by proxy.

the victim of this illness. In Boath's research men reported
that their lives were disrupted – their work was affected,
their sense of peace at home disturbed, they were involved
in extra work managing the home, the income that the
woman might have had was lost and they felt acutely the
pressure of living with a depressed person who could not
cope.

These findings raise important questions about what
exactly is the burden of care placed on the non-depressed
members of the family and support network. Why are the
household and childcare tasks seen to be women's responsibilities? Much of this is because of popular beliefs about
gender roles. It is also about a gross underestimation of
what new motherhood entails. If the woman does not
manage to cope with her usual workload, why do other
family members see themselves as victims rather than
erstwhile beneficiaries? The judgement placed upon a
woman when she is experiencing some degree of PND
depends upon her ability to function in these arenas. By

defining the problem for the father of the baby as being one 'caused' by caring for the mother and coping with that which she no longer manages to do, the fact that he might actually be suffering directly from the same things as the new mother is obscured. It is important to understand that the difference between the mother and other family members is that she physically conceived, became pregnant, gave birth and (possibly) breastfed the infant. There may have been temporary and marginal biological factors that impacted upon her physical comfort and health. The financial worries, broken nights, childcare concerns, domestic burdens and other everyday matters that have been influenced by the new baby impact directly upon the entire family unit. The mother is not (or at least should not) be treated and seen as the sole recipient of change caused by the arrival of the new family member.

Indeed, some of the men involved with the women I talked to behaved in bizarre ways and were unable to cope – not with having to care for a depressed woman – but with having had a baby. So part of the conundrum that makes up this paradox is that women and men have parallel experiences. Women get pathologised for being depressed after childbirth – although there are sound and logical reasons why they might. Men, on the other hand, get blamed if they do not take on a supportive role, but, if they do, they themselves experience distress – not only because they are helping a depressed person, but because they are having equivalent experiences to the mother.

Women's rage: gender relations or PND by proxy?

Throughout the discussions with all the women I interviewed, there was an undercurrent of rage. They were angry with the midwives, doctors, hospital policies, way they were treated, their own bodies, their own behaviours, their circumstances, the losses they experienced and their failure to deal with that rage. Far from feeling guilty and a burden to their partners, many of them expressed fury at the man for not being prepared to change while they themselves do the work and make the compromises.

Despite the positive view that most of the respondents had had about their partners prior to the birth, there were many ways in which they felt let down by them. Jane's case is typical. She told of a difficult day when she was exhausted because the baby had been particularly tired and irritable. Her fiancé went out for a drink with his friends and did not return till four in the morning. That was the first time. Since then he frequently went out and came home very late, saying that he did not think that the baby should change his life.

More subtly, Francis's husband told her she was not a good mother, a role in life she would not have chosen if it had not been for his insistence. He was very good at handling the children and criticised the way she coped with them. This eroded her confidence, which had diminished anyway since the birth of the second baby.

In Matilda's case, her husband had been abroad and not returned until several weeks after the birth. She felt very angry with him because of this, although she felt guilty about doing so:

I felt very proud that I'd managed on my own without him at all. On the other hand, whenever she cried I tended to 'throw her' in his direction and say 'change her!'. He thinks I'm just nagging him.

Shirley's partner slowly withdrew from his original promise to look after the baby. She felt overall he was

generally supportive, but his share of the tasks slipped off
in the course of the six months after the birth:

> *I think if Mike and I have arguments it will be
> about the baby – probably I'll get more irritated
> if he doesn't take an interest.*

Wendy's husband invited his brother to stay with them
shortly after she arrived home:

> *they're both out at work and I cook the evening
> meal. And they just sit around drinking coffee
> and talking in the evenings. They don't help with
> the washing up or anything like that. I was
> thinking 'should I carry on feeling resentful or
> should I do something?'*

She later declared that she had totally lost her faith in
men. Natasha's partner was also apparently uncommitted
to giving her support. At first, he played with the baby,
but after a few weeks he started going out which made her
feel very low in spirit. This situation got worse, and by six
months she was really fed up because she was stuck at
home and he could go out for a drink straight from work
and she did not know when to expect him home:

> *I may be silly, but sometimes I think he just wants
> me to be stuck in all day. His life hasn't changed.
> He's got to do overtime, but I think 'anything to get
> out of the house and he's happy!'*

At the time of the last interview, he rarely played with the
baby, told her he was unsure whether marriage to each

other was a good idea because she was so possessive, and he would not even babysit to allow her to go out or be alone, even for short periods.

Sylvia found her husband 'thrilled' over the baby but not supportive to her:

> *He sort of accepts that I'm ratty and tired because I don't get a chance to rest or do anything. He doesn't do anything positive to counter it. Occasionally he does. Eventually he'll say 'well, I'll prepare supper' rather than 'don't worry about supper, I'll prepare it'. In other words, he'll say 'do you want me to prepare supper?' if it looks as if he's not going to get his dinner!*

Meg's husband looked after the children while she was ill, but stopped more or less doing anything once she had recovered. He did however, encourage her to nap at weekends:

> *the interesting thing about Brian is the couple of times I've been out and left him with the baby he's jibbed at changing the nappies. Last night, I said 'look there he is. I've cleaned his bottom, there's a nappy, put it on. Then I'll give you something to eat.'*

Boyd and Sellers, who conducted a survey on the *British Way of Birth*[3], spend several pages quoting letters from women and some from men about their reactions to pregnancy, birth and the early postnatal weeks. Some of their respondents made the point that men are equally responsible for the baby coming into the world. But they failed to indicate that this responsibility had consequences.

Surely equal responsibility means equal work? But no – in this case the message they offered their readers was that this meant that men should not be made to feel 'left out'. They quote Derek:

There is one point, however, we are disappointed about: the survey was only addressed to the mother, not to the father as well. It is a fact of life that it takes two people to produce a child, why exclude the father in the care of it.[3]

His wife Silkie, apparently in support of his view and the way he conducted his role, says:

It is a matter of our convenience that my husband goes out to earn the money and I look after household and child. But this does not mean that our baby would be as healthy as it is without the support of his father. If my husband did not care about our child, I would have had a rotten time during pregnancy, because he might not be willing to put up with my tiredness and bad moods. If he had not cared for our unborn child, he would not have supported me in suffering pains during pregnancy rather than taking painkillers, which might have damaged the child (that meant a bad-tempered wife for him). He might not give me a helping hand when I am worn out through breast-feeding. He would just say 'put him on the bottle, then you will be less exhausted and more fun for me'. Surely the husband is a major factor in the well-being of the baby, a healthy pregnancy, a healthy birth and a healthy child.[4]

The authors comment that they have included Silkie and Derek's comments in full in order to represent 'the feelings of those couples who approach childbirth in a spirit of equality'.[5] But where is equality? Where is the concern for the woman – the mother of the child in this image? While no one has the right to proclaim to know exactly what Silkie herself means, there seems to be a undertone in this quotation in which she portrays herself as an invisible martyr. Her use of terms such as 'suffering' pain and 'worn out' breastfeeding, allied with encouragement by Derek to persevere with the actions leading to these conditions, hit home. She is identifying his care as that for the (male) child, whereas she herself seems desperate for love and attention.

Silkie's words here correspond in detail to the anger expressed by many of the women I interviewed. Data from the *That's Life* survey further endorse their accounts, particularly their experiences with the babies' fathers. Some women were positive about the fathers, although never without qualification. In these cases, men were presented as potentially supportive but not really up to the role of full-time carer:

> *For a man he's great. But I think no man can ever really understand just what a woman feels and experiences at this time.*[6]

> *I couldn't have got through the birth without him and I can't imagine how I'll cope when he goes back to sea (although I will!).*[7]

Very few of the fathers, with the women I spoke to, met their partners' expectations in relation to emotional support and child- care, which in certain cases (such as Penelope, Wendy and Isobel) was a significant factor in making the women depressed and anxious. But is the man's withdrawal an indication of tension and a way of avoiding further distress.

The fathers do not allow the existence of a baby to make long-term changes to their lives. It is women whose lives have to change. It is the women then who have to manage not only the practical (hard as they are) tasks surrounding baby and childcare; they have to manage (or be deemed responsible for) the emotions that accompany such fundamental changes for the whole family.

The baby's father is essential, of course, to the overall process of having a baby; but for a man to father in the sense of taking child rearing as one of his day-to-day priorities might require him to re-negotiate a sense of subjective masculinity. To be recognised as being able to father a child, through inseminating a woman, reinforces masculinity, but despite beliefs about the 'new man' this image upholds another myth. Disruption and change of lifestyle, which caring for a baby demands, leads to what Peter Marris calls a 'breakdown of interpretative structure' which may only be redeemed by the imposition of a new structure which brings with it new habits of thought.[8] For a man this would involve re-thinking their sense of masculinity and what it is reasonable to do as a man; while for women it is seen to be the natural progression into fulfilled femininity – motherhood. Thus, the day-to-day routine of childcare reinforces the differences between men and women's lives and underpins the social construction of femininity and masculinity.

The complex web of the vicious circle in which relationships change with the arrival of a baby are subject to interpretation by everyone who hears the personal stories of strife and distress. Pregnancy and birth are obvious times of transition for the mother involved. But what happens to the father? Popular images suggest he becomes proud and a bit incompetent.

As Charlie Lewis's[9] study showed, men come into their
own, particularly in the fun areas of child-rearing. But
how do they cope with the strains of the early days and
weeks of parenting? Why should it be assumed they are
rocks?

What do women expect?

All the women I spoke to were asked to tell me about their
expectations of their partner in the role of the new father.
All discussed in detail the way that their partners were
affected by the postnatal period. On the whole, the
women believed their partners would be excellent
fathers. In this they meant that they would share household tasks and baby care, while making efforts to maintain
the relationship with themselves and other children, if
there were any. In reality, some came through with
flying colours, particularly the partners of Melanie,
Lynn, Angela, Jerri and Samantha. Despite their depression, Angela, Jerri and Samantha all agreed that their
experiences would have been far deeper and more
prolonged if it were not for their partners. They were
supported not only in childcare and domestic tasks but
also in themselves. They were told they were wonderful –
their partners remained on their side all along. There did
not seem to be any question that these men were doing
anyone a favour.

Three men, however, went completely off course. It
was difficult to talk to Penelope, Wendy and Isobel
without feeling the antipathy provoked by the stories
they told of their partner's behaviour. However, it was
also clear that these men were undergoing personal
stress – a PND by proxy?

Penelope's story

This is really the story of Roger who suffered from depression and frequently drank too much. He was also scared of commitment and had extreme ambivalent feelings from the time of pregnancy until nine months after the birth. His story then perhaps is PND by proxy, because of pre-existing risk factors. Penelope was 41 when I met her. She had been married briefly when she was in her twenties, and, some time after that marriage broke up, she met another man whom she lived with for four years. They broke up when she found out he had been having an affair for a number of years with a mutual friend. 'They'd known each other for a very long time – they'd worked together. So initially I thought I could cope. But he wouldn't go. I had made a bad mistake in economic terms – making him joint owner [of the house she had had before they met].' He had also used the house as collateral for a business venture that had not gone well. Thus, at the end of that relationship, in her late thirties, she had financial problems and was living alone and feeling very down:

The only way I could cope with it was to go right back into my shell. I also decided I had submerged my own interests – I'd supported him emotionally and financially – and was very hurt for a long time. I looked about ten years older than I should have done, was very fat and didn't like myself very much.

Through the help of supportive friends she lost weight, regained her energy and self-esteem and began to enjoy her working and social life again. Eighteen months after the break-up she met Roger, whom she described as her current partner and who is the father of her baby. However, he was married. Penelope had never had a relationship with a married man and believed him when he said that if it had not been for his children he would have left his wife a long time ago:

> *That was a very difficult year. I found that I was beginning to neglect college work to respond to Roger's needs. His relationship with his wife was poor. They had terrible rows about the children and he was on the verge of becoming an alcoholic. But on another level we found we could talk to each other. We found an intellectual meeting that was very important.*

They stopped seeing each other for a while when Roger's wife discovered their affair. Some time later, while Penelope was having a relationship with another man whom she also saw as needing emotional support, she and Roger met by chance. He moved out from his family home into a flat and they began their relationship again:

> **Paula:** *Can I just stop you there? The significant men in your life all seem to need emotional support. Why do you choose them?*

> **Penelope:** *[Laugh] I don't know – I've thought about this a lot ... It goes back to one's childhood I suppose. My mother particularly extolled the virtues of self-sacrifice. And I suppose that model has rubbed off on me.*

*That idea that one should serve other people is
very strong.*

Penelope had suffered a great deal from depression as an
adolescent. Much of this was caused by low self-esteem as
she did not consider herself attractive. 'I'd compare
myself unfavourably with other people. At the same
time, I knew I could do some things better than others.'

The relationship with Roger grew and she became
pregnant. She was very pleased. She found that Roger
became very involved in her pregnancy, particularly the
pre-natal testing for Down's syndrome. 'It was a scientific
problem – so he was fascinated.'

*I also felt it was important for him to see the scans.
We'd had a long talk about it. I said he didn't have
to stay with me if he couldn't cope. But when we saw
the consultant – he was about Roger's age – they
communicated instantly and he relaxed totally. He
got sort of involved in the research aspects of it. It
was slightly male chauvinism. They thought they
were talking about interesting scientific phenomena.
After the amniocentesis he got very supportive. He'd
seen Leah on the monitor and he named her – which
was very interesting.*

She felt optimistic both about becoming a mother and her
expectations of Roger as a father and partner. However,
when I visited her the second time, things had changed
dramatically. The baby was three months old (having
been born seven and a half weeks prematurely) and the

relationship between Penelope and Roger had taken a
serious knock because of his conduct.

Seven months into her pregnancy, Penelope started to
bleed. She was terrified that she might lose the baby,
dialled the emergency services and went directly to the
hospital. She was kept in for four days and then discharged from hospital. A few days later, she had a
discharge, and, despite medical advice to rest, it did not
cease:

> It was a nice hot day. Roger had been in a state of
> depression – which was getting worse. I was very
> concerned. We were having lunch in the garden and
> he was overloaded with work from the office. I
> suddenly realised I was bleeding again. I felt quite
> calm and rang the hospital. They said come in. Off
> I went.

She was told she would have to stay in because her waters
had broken. Roger was upset because they had planned a
summer holiday camping in France. They were taking
Roger's children from his marriage with them. He was
cross that Penelope had to be admitted, as he wanted
her in France. When she was admitted to hospital that
second time, she went into labour almost immediately.
Roger arrived at the end, 'just as they were fiddling with
the placenta'. He seemed to be 'dazed' by the baby's
arrival. He had refused to go to hospital with her as he
thought 'I was putting it on'. The midwife, who phoned to
tell him to come in, asked Penelope whether he was always
like that as he had been offhand with her. Penelope had
had a very hard time in the maternity unit – the baby was
in special care, she had problems expressing milk and was
suffering from her episiotomy scarring. She was also
worried about the baby's health. Roger went with his

oldest children to France, just when she felt she most needed his support:

> *I felt totally demoralised. I really needed his support. I didn't know where he was. We'd had one postcard. I felt I had a lot of decisions to make on my own and didn't feel very strong about taking them.*

She thought that the baby's prematurity was the result of stress. Roger had been getting more and more depressed which placed increasing demands on Penelope. 'He used to come through the front door being totally miserable and I thought "God, I can't cope with this". He couldn't say what was wrong but I thought it was at least in part because the baby was coming'. He accused her of trapping him by getting pregnant.

Her discharge from hospital with the baby was supported by friends because no one knew where Roger was. The house was absolutely filthy – he had left it in chaos. Penelope still 'didn't know where the hell he was', and felt she was 'going batty' because she needed to make decisions about the baby and had to do it alone.

Because the baby had been so premature she had no baby things at home and there were two cats that she felt she couldn't deal with. Friends helped her clear up and then Roger arrived home. Penelope exhausted herself in looking after the baby and gradually cleaning the house. 'He didn't actually realise she needed a lot of care and in the end we had a fearsome row.' Penelope became very stressed and depressed with all she had to do but 'Roger doesn't see it as his role if I can't cope at 2 a.m. to get up – and I find that devastating'. There had been a recent occasion when his children had been at the house and the baby wouldn't stop crying, Penelope was exhausted and took the baby into bed with her. She then realised the nappy needed changing and asked Roger to change it. He said 'no'.

The story continued in this way and around the baby's sixth month Roger left home. By the time of my last interview, he had returned. His older children also seemed to spend most of their spare time at Penelope's house. Looking back at his behaviour during the birth and the following months, she felt she had never felt so isolated and despairing. 'I felt very angry towards him. He could have done so much more at one level – but Leah was an awful shock to him and he was terrified of commitment and everything else. I don't know whether I will ever trust him again.'

Wendy's story

Dave and Wendy had been married for four years when she became pregnant, but their relationship had not been smooth. Although they had decided to divorce shortly before Wendy discovered she was pregnant, they were both happy about the prospect of parenthood together.

Dave came from a conservative rural background while Wendy's family were middle-class intellectuals. Her sisters married men who were both wealthier and more successful than they were, while Dave and Wendy both worked for local government with Wendy having a more senior role. There was some opposition to her marriage from her family and some from Dave's for slightly different reasons:

I made a conscious decision in the sort of man I wanted to marry. I wanted to marry someone who was not a businessman flying round the world. Not a doctor − or someone going to spend a lot of time away from home. And I'm pleased now that I've made that choice.

Wendy believed that Dave 'was more excited than I am at the news [of the baby]. Not that I'm not enthusiastic − but he's getting really excited.' Wendy was very aware that the new baby would create a great deal of extra work for her because she wanted to return to work as soon as she could. She believed, from their discussions, that Dave would take his share of the load. 'He's already started to help me with the shopping and he's chucking things in washing machines occasionally.' She felt guilty about expecting him to do this 'but that will rub off quite easily [laugh]'.

When Wendy and Dave married, he had a serious drink problem. He gradually drank less as their relationship progressed and Dave's family said that Wendy had been the only person who had ever been able to help him. However, Dave would also have episodes of withdrawal which might have been depression. Sometimes these were severe.

We had had a row for some reason − and he didn't say anything to me for a fortnight. Not a word. Even though I'd come in here and start speaking to him. It freaked me out. I went to stay with my parents. I was very distressed and distraught about it and when I came back he still didn't speak.

What she soon discovered was that he had started drinking again. Although Wendy could switch off from the situation when she was at work, she used to dread going home at night.

> *I was concerned and cared about him – it was just terrible ... I hate myself sometimes because in a situation like that he thinks I'm a snotty, goody-goody who never drinks extensively – really pretty boring.*

He eventually started to attend Alcoholics Anonymous meetings three times a week and things improved.

Just after the baby arrived though, Dave returned to his bad behaviour. He offered me coffee when I arrived, but was very gruff, and I found it difficult to understand what he was saying as he had a broad accent which was a strange contrast to the articulate, middle-class Wendy.

Dave was there all through the birth and she found him very supportive and the labour was reasonably short and the baby healthy. Dave took two weeks off work for paternity leave, but he spent it all working on the reno-vation of the house, and because Wendy had neither the time nor the energy (and probably not the inclination) to get involved in this she hardly saw him over this period. 'I felt quite alone then, really.' Dave reacted badly to the baby:

> **Wendy:** *I think she freaked him out a bit. He couldn't bear to hear her cry. He got frustrated and annoyed that he couldn't do anything to help her and that made him ratty. Her cries haven't worried me at all.*
>
> **Paula:** *So he's more ratty than you?*

Wendy: *Oh, yes, yes! And, umm, I find that, although I am tired, it doesn't really affect me mood-wise.*

He was also, however, behaving in a totally inconsiderate way – his brother was staying and Wendy had to cook and clean up after them. 'They just sit around drinking coffee and talking in the evenings.'

One day, she told them that she saw no reason why she should do the cooking when she was looking after the baby. 'I felt very angry but Dave was very angry at me for saying that.' When Wendy returned to work after three months, they hired a nanny which made things a little easier for her. She stopped breastfeeding which meant that Dave sometimes got up in the night to feed the baby. But when that happened: 'He moans all the next day about how tired he is. It's not worth it.'

She felt that Dave found life hard and that had always been the case, but the problems with their relationship before the pregnancy were exacerbated by the shock of what parenthood meant – particularly for Dave.

Even now, sometimes I think 'oh, that selfish sod' – but I'd be unhappy without him. And really I should concentrate on the times when I am happy.

Wendy firmly believed that any episodes of depression she had had since the baby was born were because of Dave's behaviour, not the baby directly:

The baby has highlighted his priorities. He doesn't prioritise in the way I would. Whereas I would put him and her first, sometimes he won't put us first. But if you sit and talk to him, he will explain his priorities and in a roundabout way, he does. But I don't have anyone else so I have to accept it.

Isobel's story

Isobel was a health-care professional. Tough minded, clear about her value system, formal in her relationship with me at the first meeting and appeared to be a very organised person. Isobel saw herself as independent: 'I don't feel I need a lot of people; if I want talk to anyone about things I talk to my husband.'

She had been married to Graham, a teacher, for four years and the baby had been planned and provisions made for maternity leave. They had moved from Scotland to London where house prices were high, and she felt that the two-bedroom flat they now owned was not really good enough for them: 'We want to move on to better things.' She believed that both of them were ready to settle down when they met, as they had travelled and established their professional qualifications.

Isobel described their social life as mainly consisting of home entertaining among a small circle of friends. 'I think we're moving towards a different form of socialising. I see my friends during the day, at work or whatever and my husband when I come home from work.'

She said that, while they shared household chores equally, she did most of the gardening because Graham didn't like doing it. 'But he dish-washes and does the car.' After the baby, she anticipated that they would both have to do more:

If I'm feeding the baby then I would expect my husband to do some of the jobs that I would

otherwise be doing. Umm ... he's terribly enthus-
iastic about changing nappies, etc. so I've no par-
ticular worries as far as that's concerned. He's not
terribly keen about getting up during the night. And
I've got to get up to feed the baby anyway ... and
he's got a job to go to the next day.

Both Graham and Isobel were pleased that they had a
boy – which is what they had both wanted. When labour
started, Isobel felt calm but Graham was 'panicky'.

Isobel was in hospital for four days during which
time Graham tiled the bathroom and put some finishing
touches to the kitchen so she would have a nice surprise
when she arrived home. However, 'to be honest, I was in a
daze and it all washed over me. I had to make an effort to
be interested so he wouldn't be upset.' Isobel's mother
was staying with them to help for a week, then Graham
was home for the half-term week. Isobel found the
childcare hard once she was on her own, and the baby
needed feeding every three hours. 'He's dreadful in the
evenings ... my husband is still cooking the evening meal
and baths the baby.'

Sometimes at night when I'm so exhausted and the
baby is crying, I just don't want to know. Then
he'll [Graham] take him so he is out of earshot –
and Graham gets him to go to sleep.

When the baby was three months old, for the first time
Isobel looked pleased to see me, rather than dutifully
taking part in the research as she had done on the first
two occasions. She described their life as having 'got
very complicated'. Their old cat had been killed and,
very much against Isobel's wishes, Graham had arrived

home with two kittens. She was worried that they would scratch the baby and about possible infections, and had become very agitated and angry with him for seeming so inconsiderate. She said that, although that had been the first 'stress thing', she realised it had been building up for some time. It was then that I realised it was Graham she was talking about:

> The baby 'started crying from 2.00 p.m. until midnight and from midnight until 2 in the morning. This was the source of friction ... We both took turns in coming through here [to the living room] – we were both getting fractious and missing out on an awful lot of sleep. My husband in particular because he was terribly worried about the neighbours – the people down below but I said 'so what? I don't care'. But this caused friction and there was obviously a lot of tension building up with my husband around that time. If either of us had postnatal depression – it was him [laugh]!

Graham became increasingly hostile to Isobel and one morning at 2 a.m. he:

> started throwing nappy pins across the room at me and several of them were bent, and he threw them with the intention of hitting me. I was quite taken aback as he had never done anything like that in his life before. And then another night – he was trying to watch something on TV and I had gone to the toilet and he said 'are you going to take this child?' It was grossly unfair – I had taken about 5 minutes out of hours and hours of crying.

Some weeks later, he was arrested late at night for drink-driving and had to call her from the police station. He had been prone to depression in the past, and Isobel felt that, because of the baby, things had been getting on top of him. She felt it had not been relevant to tell me before 'but we have had some difficulties in the past. But he seems to have been OK for some time until now.' The family doctor had signed Graham off work for a month. 'I realised I had to be strong now. Until then he was very supportive and maybe he's had this fit of depression because I've been expecting too much of him.'

She constantly wondered if she had caused his depression in this way. Graham was withdrawing from her, and she was having to give up caring for herself and doing any housework in order to cope with the baby and with Graham. As Isobel's birthday came due (they would normally go out for a meal and celebrate), she kept asking what they should do:

> *I wasn't getting any response. He was off school but helping out a friend doing some labouring which was therapeutic. He came in and said 'I'm not going to be able to get you much for your birthday this year.' Anyway, as we were short of money, I had already accepted that I wasn't going to get a big present. But what upset me terribly was that the evening before my birthday he had obviously not even got me anything. I wouldn't have minded even a box of chocolates or a pair of tights. But he'd come home with nothing. I wasn't going to be able to open a present in the morning.*

When I met Isobel for the last time, when the baby was six months old, things had gradually settled down for her. The baby was sleeping more during the night, the incessant crying had stopped and she felt she had a little more time to herself. Graham was feeling slightly better, but did complain that Isobel always put the baby before him 'although he understands that's the way it's got to be I think'. Isobel had given Graham some serious pep talks about his role when she returns to work, and she thought that he would try and pull his weight, although she did describe him as a 'fair-weather' father. The whole experience had made her feel older, slightly more cynical about her relationship with Graham, although she was pleased that she had managed to remain strong and able to cope through the crises. However, it wasn't yet all behind her as she felt that she was 'just managing to keep her head above water – just managing to cope with everyday'.

Understanding PND by proxy?

Figure 4, showing the burden of parenthood, speaks for itself. Men and women are under pressure when they have a baby. While women are prepared by health professionals to expect to lose sleep and energy and to put baby care first, men are treated differently. The health-care professionals pay attention to the role of the father and mostly encourage men to come to parenting classes. Fathers are expected to provide social support 'for the mother', whereas they themselves have also undergone a trauma and life change for which they are probably less well prepared than their partners.

Challenging the paradox and getting on with your life

Introduction

Many women get distressed or depressed after childbirth, even if it is just for a few tearful hours. Most have several days of feeling down in between days and weeks of feeling all right. Sometimes there are days of tremendous happiness. The pressure of childcare and the burdens of domestic and work responsibilities, as well as changes in family and friendship patterns, guarantee that most of us will need good support to avoid falling victim to a series of low moods. The best survival strategy is to ensure that the low moods, distress and intermittent depression *do not last too long*. If they join up, severe clinical depression might set in and that is more difficult to shift. A major factor in avoiding prolonged depression is to find a way, however small, of *taking control* of your life.

It seems amazing, looking back, but most people's experience confirms that the main *risk* of falling foul of these black moods occurs over the first six postnatal months. A very short period in the overall scheme of your life. But as your live it over the hours without a good night's sleep, with physical discomfort, a poor self-image, a partner who himself feels the strain and without time to yourself, the world seems an unfamiliar and sometimes hostile place. That changes. Emotional and physical scars heal, routines emerge and there is time for pleasure and relaxation. A small minority of people never fully recover – the strain may have proved too much for their relationship. They may find that they have lost their ability or the will to carry on with the work or career they had once cherished. They never manage to re-capture the physical size and shape they once were. But for most women, with some support and a little self-help, life becomes more enjoyable. You return to the person you once were – with added value. You have a(nother) child and you have demonstrated to yourself and everyone else that you could meet the challenges you had to face.

You recognise who you are but you have also become someone else. Your experience has become integrated into your life and the way you conduct your relationships, and you know more about yourself and your powers. Re-integration and change are an essential part of our lives. We may mourn what we have lost and left behind, but we are more in command of what lies ahead (Figure 5). Understanding the psychological processes which are an inevitable consequence of life events, such as childbirth and motherhood, is halfway to taking control of them.

Taking control: when and how?

Taking control is not the same as trying to put something out of your mind. Sometimes, the images of the person

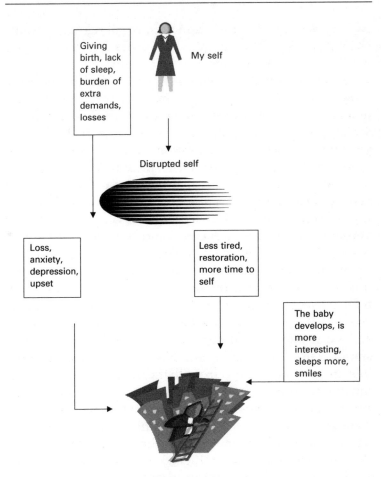

Figure 5 The transition to the renewed self.

who keeps a 'stiff upper lip' or the 'control freak', being 'uptight', not taking your own or other people's pain seriously are assumed to be what psychologists mean by taking control of your life. In fact, it is almost the opposite. Taking control of your life is about self-awareness and understanding. You are aware of your reactions, behaviours, emotions and feelings. You *recognise, accept*

and pay attention to them. You become increasingly familiar with what you want and what is best for you, and you
work towards those goals.

It is important to have a constant self-awareness. Self-
awareness means that you remain aware of what is
happening to you despite, and especially, when things
are rough. For instance, many of the women I met told
me that they had no idea how depressed they had been
until they looked back at some of the things they had done
or some of the things that had happened to them. They
had no idea that they had felt so low, or allowed certain
things to build up. *However, the point is that they did.* If
you lose your self-awareness, you lose your awareness of
who and where you are in the complex web of your life.

All lives are complicated much of the time. We are a
mixture of our physical and mental make-up – which, in
turn, have emerged from our genetic and social backgrounds. Others react to us as they see and perceive us,
and we make sense of our lives according to our understanding of how others respond to us. It is almost impossible to get your mind around the range of factors that
influence your life and emotional state at any one time.
We have all experienced that loss of self-awareness. We
sometimes chose to do so – you might think it's time you
had a wild night out with your friends. But that is a choice.
It is very different from letting anyone, who wants to, take
advantage of you or hitting the bottle because you don't
like the way things are going for you.

Having a baby is hard work! Losing sleep and time for
reflection and losing the everyday routines that you took
for granted place you at risk of losing control and self-
awareness.

Few of us get through the transition to motherhood
unscathed. Many of us experience life events that are
completely unrelated to becoming a mother. Nevertheless, they may seriously impact upon your mental well-

being. The women I talked to included several who had experienced bereavement and illness among their loved ones during the postnatal months. Some had been ill themselves, and one or two of the partners/fathers had problems related to their work. Life goes on. What is important to understand though is that self-awareness and taking control *enable us to cope* in the best way we can. Self-awareness around feelings and mood, when depression and anxiety creep upon us, can prevent the depression from becoming severe.

The keys to control and self-awareness are social support and physical and emotional fitness.

Social support

This is easier for some to achieve than for others. If you get along with your parents or other relatives and they are able to support you, that is a bonus and highly beneficial. Some women had no idea just how good their sister or mother could be, until they had had their babies and received their support. Unfortunately, some had problems they could not foresee, and discovered that the person who was supposed to be most supportive was in fact a liability. The support provided by the baby's father, as we have seen, can be brilliant or disastrous. Some new mothers have friends in similar positions to themselves, while others feel very isolated.

Taking control means recognising that you will (and do) need support at various stages in the postnatal months.

While social support is essential for maintenance of mental well-being, there are several times and events that leave you feeling down or low. This is when you might need help to take control and maintain your sense of self-awareness.

Emotional fitness

Feelings of anxiety, panic, uncertainty and depression are all part of the human condition, and many experts argue that they have a purpose. For instance, episodes of depression can sometimes lead us to contemplation and restoration – simply by forcing us to retreat and make a short separation from the pressures of life. You can grow through the depression because it can lead you to a more realistic sense of what you might achieve. Depression slows you down and thus may prevent you over-extending yourself physically and mentally. When certain systems shut down, your metabolism slows and you rest. However, depression also involves stress, anxiety and panic. There are two ways that depression prevents you having control over your life. It is self-awareness that enables you to *process* your moods and experiences to make sense of what is happening. In order to do this, it is necessary to understand some possible reasons for feelings getting out of control and how a sense of self-awareness might help us regain that control.

1.   What is underneath everyday awareness?

Self-awareness may be achieved through an in-depth understanding of the origins of the emotions and feelings, thus placing them in the context in which they belong. This is unlikely to be the 'here and now'. Some emotions lurk in the unconscious mind, and influence us sometimes when we are least expecting them and we certainly don't always understand where they come from. For instance, if you feel you have so much to do, too little time to do it in and you also wonder if your partner and friends still care about you, it is difficult to take control. You may simply sink and feel pain. But that pain may be the pain from similar feelings from far earlier in your life. Your parents were demanding – they wanted you to be perfect. They wanted you to achieve in school academically, in sports, become an accomplished musician and help them around the home. The demands came all at once. They didn't give you a sense of priorities and paid no attention to *your* needs and unique abilities. You reacted physically by doing everything – working hard with never any time to think or to be *in control of your own life*. You didn't recognise what was most important either to them or to you. You didn't know when you had done well because the pressure never ceased. You were only as good as the things you hadn't finished doing.

The pressures surrounding new motherhood may bring back those feelings – the parents in your head, making unrealistic demands that you never fulfilled. In fact, you are still trying to fulfil their demands and please them because you have never learned to please yourself. You don't know how to prioritise. Panic and stress spirals into depression when your mind and body give up trying to cope with the overload.

How do you decide whether a feeling relates to the present or the past? Try asking yourself some simple but searching questions. If you have the time and space, you could write the questions and the answers down:

- *What were your feelings when you experienced pressure as a child?*
- *Who met your needs when you were pressured?*
- *What would you have wanted them to do to help you?*
- *Did you always feel valued?*

Thinking about the answers to these questions, and how they also relate to your current situation, might help you separate some of the feelings into those that belong to 'now' and those that are emerging to meet familiar stresses.

2.   Do you see the world through dark glasses

Many of us experience ourselves and the outside world in negative ways. We have thoughts that pick out the worst aspects of every scenario and continue to develop our perceptions from behind dark glasses. The impossible demands made by our parents did not only instil the feelings of panic which emerge from our unconscious, but on a very conscious level we are aware of just how poor our performance may be. The way we were described in the past, in relation to the standards that were set, stay with us. We failed to achieve what was expected of us. We fell below the required standards. We never managed to live up to the ideal set by our parents and *adopted later by ourselves*. Some parents were not only critical of you and the way you didn't live up to their expectations. They compared you unfavourably with others – your sisters, brothers or your school friends. There are times now when you hate other people – the mothers you know from the clinic or your friends in high-powered jobs.

You know they are making a better job of their lives and motherhood than you. That is the way it has always been and there is no reason to believe that that isn't the case now. When did you ever do anything well? If these thoughts and impossible standards live with you, then, whenever there is pressure, you will evaluate yourself and what you do in a negative way. That will bring you down.

It is a simple but interesting exercise to see all the things you perceive as negative in reverse:

- *learn to check yourself when you have negative thoughts;*
- *turn them around and feel positive (don't think about what you haven't done – feel pleased about what you have done);*
- *spend a little time each day concentrating on your good points and comparing yourself to others in a positive way.*

Finding the help you need

PND happens in the context of parenthood, of course, which means you have to consider the baby as well as yourself when understanding your emotions and seeking the solutions. The importance of social support has been discussed and remains important, even if more expert support is required. Without practical and emotional support on a daily basis, it is difficult to find the strength and time to deal with the underlying problems and become self-aware.

There are two particularly useful psychotherapeutic approaches to defeating depression and anxiety, and both emphasise the importance of changing the way you think about yourself and the world around you. The first is cognitive–analytic therapy and the second cognitive–behavioural therapy. Both have overlaps and both focus on 'cognitions' or ways that we think. There are now many recognised experts in each approach who offer therapy on a 'time-limited' basis. There is evidence from formal evaluations of these approaches that, by clearly defining a problem, it is possible for the client and the therapist/counsellor to work to that focus in an effective way, which leaves the client able to have a different perspective on their world and a different approach to their everyday behaviours and thoughts. This will enable them to change the aspects of their lives that were causing so much distress.

Cognitive–analytic therapy (CAT)

This is a time-limited, integrated psychotherapy. Clients and therapists proceed with the treatment in a formal way – the client having to complete some basic questions about their emotional and cognitive perspectives on themselves and their social relationships. The process over the (approximately) 18 sessions involves mutual, written feedback and a final re-evaluation of progress on the identified problems. Because CAT combines both cognitive (the way we think and process information) and psychodynamic (attention to the unconscious) elements, it requires the client to focus upon their early relationships and identify how they impact upon their contemporary emotions and thought patterns.

The formal written feedback at set stages enables clients, after the sessions have ceased, to work further on their emotional development and change. A basic focus then of this approach is upon the self in relation to the social world, including what perceptions the individual has of her self. By talking through some situations that are occurring in a person's life, in the context of the pre-identified perceptions that the individual uses to structure their world, it is possible to identify ways to change your thinking, your emotional reactions and related behaviours. This method of psychotherapy enables you to have some understanding of the early relationships in your life that formed you and your perceptions in the way they are today. You learn why you respond to circumstances by being depressed and how you might find a way beyond these patterns. By focusing on emotional reactions as well, the individual also comes to recognise how they feel and take control in ways they might not have been able to do previously.

Cognitive–behavioural therapy (CBT)

CBT is more widely available than CAT at present in the UK, although both are gaining popularity. CBT combines behavioural treatments (i.e. those that help us change some of the ways we do things) and cognitive ones. It is very prescribed, and therapists refer to the treatment as a 'package'. Sessions involve structured tasks and achieving set goals and there is no significant opportunity to talk in an unstructured way. The main focus of this type of therapy is called *cognitive re-structuring*. This is essentially a means of making an individual rethink the way they view the world – particularly the issues that are causing the distress. Sometimes the sessions involve 'exposure' to the cause of the distress – which in some cases, such as those of phobias, the person might gradually and systematically be exposed to their phobia (e.g. heights, spiders), while being encouraged to think in a positive manner about the object of fear. In the case of depression, the package usually focuses upon cognitive restructuring alone. Thus the individual would have to think through and articulate the way they think about certain relevant situations in their life and change the way they think about them (e.g. some women I spoke to managed to re-think their reactions to undone household tasks – they learned not to worry or panic about them, while others continued to feel obliged to keep an orderly and spotless household while caring for a baby). They usually failed and thus became overwhelmed by their negative thoughts.

Physical fitness

There is little doubt that being physically fit provides extra stamina and enables you to carry out the things you need to do without being totally exhausted. It also makes you feel better about yourself – it boosts your confidence and self-esteem. Being fit is good for your body and your mind. The problems, of course, are: How can I make the time to get and stay fit? What can I do when I am exhausted all the time. I don't have the energy to get fit.

There are three useful and possible ways to begin to get fit – relaxation (something that most of us neglect), stretching and toning up, and aerobic exercise. All require a time commitment – and this is an important part of the time to yourself that you need to claim. It becomes more possible to build time into most people's routines as time passes and the baby learns to play quietly, sleep longer or you feel more willing to entrust the baby to a friend or babysitter for a few hours each week.

Whatever you do to improve your physical fitness no matter how modest – enables you to cope better with anxiety and tension. It ensures that depression does not build up.

There are some simple ways of building exercise into your daily routines:

1 Walking – take the baby out in the pram for a walk at least once a day. Try to enjoy this (rather than think of it as a shopping trip that you need to get over with).

2 Relaxation – when the baby is asleep lie down. Clench every muscle as hard as you can and then let go. Try and think about your body from the toes upwards. Check there is no tension. Breathe out and in slowly. Do this for five or six minutes twice a day.

3 Self-nurturing – take time if you can to indulge yourself. Soak in a bath with sensuous oils and a luxurious foam; read a magazine and listen to your favourite music.

4 If it is possible, join a class in t'ai chi, yoga, meditation or aerobics. This may be something that could be planned before the baby is born. Daytime classes sometimes have a crèche.

Where to go from here?

When I carried out the interviews, I rejected the term PND because it implied that women's experience of depression at this stage of their lives was pathological and intrinsically linked to female biology. I argued, for these reasons and because of the diversity of my findings about women's experiences, that *PND does not exist because depression following childbirth is a rational, predictable and healthy response to loss.*

However, taking this view now, I think, risks further marginalising women's experience of the transition to motherhood and associated emotional responses. Recognising this, led me to use the term PND to describe the focus of this work. It is easier to challenge some of the views expressed by clinicians and researchers if you use a common language.

Almost without exception women get depressed to some extent when they become mothers, but the reasons for this are more complex by far than the traditional research has the power to identify. Those who do not get noticeably depressed feel the need to explain why they do not. Those who do get depressed find it easy to explain why they are. This is no surprise. Accounts of what it is like to be a mother in the early weeks, months or even years show pain and suffering as well as pleasure. And yet, mainstream researchers and clinicians are still looking for the answer to this 'illness'. The view that adaptation to motherhood for any woman is easy remains widely held. Scientists and clinicians maintain the idea that depression is pathological – they want to screen for it and act in a preventative capacity. It is in their interests to focus on the reaction as an illness, rather than recognise the diversity of responses or the tenacity and resilience of most women who experience depression as part of their individualised strategy of coping with stress, loss and change.

Postnatal depression needs to be re-conceptualised as part of the *normal experience of most women when they become mothers.* This is not the same as saying that women need to be aware that their hormones are raging after birth, to imply that mothers are irrational, or that an extraneous and dislocated set of feelings will develop. Women and men have to understand the consequences of motherhood in the context of Western industrial life in the absence of kinship networks, in the face of financial struggle, gender inequalities and gender power relations in the family.

Conclusions

Despite variations in reports and experiences, what the women I spoke to told me provides evidence to link experiences of depression in childbirth and early mothering. They are not common features of a 'syndrome' or illness, however, but associated with the shared problems surrounding the conditions of motherhood and thus expectations about the character of *women's* lives. Motherhood is tough, but so is life. No one woman's experience of mothering can be matched with another's or another of her own experiences, because lives differ. However, human beings need space, time and support to adapt to loss and change. They need help when faced with added burdens, responsibility and social isolation. This is generally acceptable it seems, in all cases, but that of becoming a mother. Depression is considered a healthy part of the process of re-integration following loss most of the time, so why is it not conceptualised in a similar way when talking about the losses following child-birth and motherhood? The ultimate myth that mother-hood is natural and desirable means that women take on its burden unconditionally.

Men, at present, are, paradoxically, seen to be psycho-logically unimpaired by the experience of becoming a father, because they are supposed to do it for status and pleasure. However, it is also clear that they are vulnerable, in similar ways to women, to the burdens placed upon in-dividuals following the transition to parenthood. Scien-tists do not ask questions about men's postnatal reactions, with a view to comparing them with those they ask about women. If they did, then the extent of women's respon-sibilities would be exposed, making it difficult to pin the label 'illness' on PND and so would highlight the extent of men's vulnerabilities to the burdens of fatherhood. Reconsideration of women's descriptions of the fathers' behaviours makes this point. Is it normal to turn to alcohol because a baby's crying prevents sleep? Is it normal for someone to carry on as before the birth with their working and social life? Is it normal *not* to become emotionally involved in the life of the infant you have just fathered?

We do not have the answers to these questions *because scientists have not asked them*. Why not? It is assumed that women will take on childcare responsibility, that they will know what to do in the infant's best interest and will continue to provide domestic support for the father. But it is not just women who choose to have children. It is not just women who have an emotional and material invest-ment in producing a family. The family, science, knowledge and myth are all products of the society in which the family exists. We all have a responsibility to understand what underpins our knowledge of taken-for-granted assumptions. It is time that psychologists and other experts asked different kinds of questions about women's mothering and the role of the scientific method in understanding and explaining PND.

Portraits of the women

Jane

Jane, originally from south London, had lived with her boyfriend for four years. He was from the Middle East, and even though they were not legally married, they had a Muslim wedding to please his family. They lived in a two-bedroom flat in London's docklands.

I first met her only three weeks before their daughter's birth. She was very smartly dressed, shy but articulate. She reported that she did not feel happy in the mornings until she had her make-up on and her hair done. She was anxious about impending motherhood, but only admitted this on the third interview. She has always seen herself as 'feminine', wanting to look pretty, and, although she wanted and expected to have children, she lacked confidence that she would be good at baby care.

Jane demonstrated a mixed picture of frustration and loneliness which was kept at bay by her satisfaction with the baby and support from her mother. Her partner was apparently ambivalent in his support and some of the positive things she said about him did not always coincide with her descriptions of his behaviour.

Lynn

Lynn had been married for nine years and they lived in a terraced house in a working-class part of London, although she herself was from a middle class family in the north of England. Her family were involved in politics, as she was herself. She described herself as 'determined', and whatever she does (including pregnancy) she throws herself into, with strong views on how it should be done. She was keen to include the baby in her life rather than build a different life around it.

She had hoped to become a mother earlier in her life, and had been trying to get pregnant for the previous seven years. She had found pregnancy 'wonderful' and had come to love the prospect of the independent midwife, she had arranged to care for her, supervising a home delivery.

However, she had had to go into hospital to have the baby because after 18 hours the midwife considered that she ought to have an epidural and speed up the contractions. She found over the following months that she needed (and received) much support from her husband and other family members.

Isobel

Isobel had been married to Graham for four years. She had left Scotland at that time to live with him in a small flat in south London. This meant she was isolated from her roots and family. However, she sees herself as an independent person who 'doesn't need to be running in and out of other people's houses'.

Isobel was formal and neat in appearance with short brown hair. She punctuated most of what she said with nervous laughter. She said that she wanted to take part in this study because she 'approved of research'. She was ambivalent about her career and wanted to have another baby fairly soon after this one. This pregnancy had been part of the couples' 'long-term plans'.

However, she found Rowan's arrival a great shock, and, although Graham was very supportive at first, he himself got very stressed and anxious about fatherhood, particularly when he couldn't stop the baby crying and didn't get enough sleep. By the time he was six months, however, Rowan cried less relentlessly and Isobel was looking forward to returning to work. They did, however, plan to leave London as soon as Graham could find a suitable teaching post.

The main change she felt in herself was that she had lost her figure and was not 'young' anymore. She said she was neither elated nor depressed: 'Just keeping my head above water. Just managing to cope with everyday life ... but I feel I've got to put effort into getting that far'.

Gwen

Gwen lived in south-west London with Stan, her husband of four years who was ten years older than her. She was well groomed, with highlighted blond hair and immaculate nails and make-up. She was assertively 'non-ambitious' in her secretarial career, although was dismissive of silly, stay-at-home women who corresponded with her image of her own mother. She wanted to confine her ambitions to family life and having a bigger and better home over the course of time. Her interests were gardening and attending to her dogs.

Gwen was concerned with her body image and had had previous episodes of putting on and losing weight in a dramatic way. The weight gain had been accompanied by depression. Thus she was particularly concerned about her pregnant body and relieved that her husband, a rugby player who was supportive of her keeping slim and fit, did not mind too much. The pregnancy had been a shock to them both, but they were reconciled in a positive way to starting a family.

Gwen herself had been born at home and, after some effort persuading various GPs in the area, managed to arrange a home delivery. However, when Hazel was born, she had a long and difficult labour, and was briefly admitted to hospital for an epidural and forceps delivery.

At the time of the third interview, she tried to stop my coming by saying she didn't have postnatal depression, although agreed in the end to tell me about her experiences anyway. She was clearly very tense and angry that Stan was not as good and supportive a father as she had hoped and expected. She did, however, want to have another child as soon as she could because: 'when all the pieces have knitted back together you can start your life again rather than have a gap. And then I think "Oh I don't have to go through all that again, do I?".'

Francis

*Francis had been married to Philip for 11 years.
They already had a five-year-old son, Roland, and
lived in a London suburb. Francis was well dressed
and made-up, and had a pleasant manner. She was
always welcoming, but, as each interview progressed,
appeared increasingly 'distracted'.*

*Listening to the tapes, I found that I was
frequently 'prompting' her while she was pausing.
Although I warmed to her, there didn't seem to be
much* rapport, *although in several ways she was
prepared to be revealing about emotional issues.*

*She had the second child for the sake of her son
and did not want any more than two children.
Initially, she had seen how friends had been tied
down with their children, but on becoming a mother
herself she had few regrets.*

*She employed a nanny after Wendy was born.
She was breastfeeding, and, although she did not like
being 'cow-like' and had some difficulties, she per-
sisted because she believed it important. Her mother
and husband had been supportive over the early days
so 'I got through my so-called postnatal depression
time without being depressed.' The feeding caused the
greatest distress, and, although Wendy was a good
baby, Roland had difficulties with the idea of a new
sister which worried Francis.*

*She found herself getting tired and with some bad
moments of depression, even when Wendy was six
months. She did not consider herself a particularly
good mother which dented her confidence: 'I feel
depressed at my apparent inadequacy'.*

Dion

Dion, a black woman born in south London, had her roots in the West Indies. However, she had several relatives including her parents living nearby. She lived with the father of her second child in a council flat in a dreary tower block, although the inside of the flat was cheerful and comfortable. She worked in a supermarket in the evenings and therefore shared childcare with her boyfriend. She didn't seem to enjoy being interviewed and continued to put her hair in rollers throughout the time I was there.

She said she did not believe her boyfriend would make a good or reliable father, particularly in relation to money, although she was really happy to be pregnant again. She was dreading the birth. 'I'm more scared than someone who's not been through it.' She was very keen to get herself back into a slim shape again afterwards.

Matilda

Matilda's baby was due three weeks before entering the third year of a four-year undergraduate course in sociology. She had been married to Desmond for 18 months, but, at the time, he was studying for a PhD in Africa. Matilda came in her teens, from Zimbabwe, as a refugee. She had had a difficult time on arriving in England, expecting white British people to be liberals, but in fact experienced racism and isolation, especially when working in Yorkshire as a nurse. She was happier being a student in London.

Two things had always been important to her — becoming a mother and becoming a professional person. She never considered choosing between career and motherhood. Thus she had looked forward to her pregnancy and becoming a mother. Matilda's pregnancy was difficult, particularly because she had to go through most of it without the support of her husband.

After the baby was born, she moved from student residences to stay with an aunt in another part of London. Her husband had not come over in time for the birth and so she handled it alone. It had been very difficult. She had been in intense pain and eventually was rushed to the operating theatre as the baby's heartbeat became weaker.

When the baby was about three months old, she was taken back to Africa by Matilda's mother, so Matilda could finish her course. Although this was traditional in her culture, and planned in advance, she had mixed feelings about it. 'I keep thinking "I must be wicked to do that to my own baby".' Ansiet her daughter was always on her mind, and she felt that being a mother had changed her and made her stronger despite the fact that she did not have her baby with her. 'My husband, friends and family seem to appreciate me more. I actually have had more energy and more determination to get on with my career.'

Samantha

Samantha was 27 and had been married to Eric, a postman, for six years. She was a supervisor in a word-processing company, and had developed a career from being an unambitious office worker. She came from a large family which had not been all that happy, partly because of poverty and a sense of being 'overcrowded', and no one had cared about education or career. Her abilities and success had isolated her from her former friends and relatives. She was constantly worried about her weight.

She was the first generation of her family to live in owner-occupied accommodation, and she and Eric had renovated a flat and then moved to the house they lived in at the time of the pregnancy. She is clear that she wants her children to have a better start in life than she perceived she had had. She had never been close to her mother and had hardly spoken to her father until she was in her teens; she found her parents to be always stressed and tired. Her relationship with her husband had been the only satisfactory one she had ever had.

She did not like Ellie when she first saw her, partly because of marks left by forceps used during delivery. She found she resented having to care for her immediately following a tiring labour. 'I thought I'd have at least one night to catch up on my sleep!'. She also had trouble with breastfeeding which she found stressful.

Gradually though, she managed to cope with the baby and loved her from very early on. Eric was very supportive and returned home early in the afternoon to take over either housework or childcare.

Three months after delivery, she had lost weight and was feeling much happier. She was also feeling more confident about returning to her office. She had attended the firm's Xmas party and was delighted to report that she had been treated like an adult person rather than a 'mother'. Although she enjoys motherhood, she would not be happy to only be at home. She adapted successfully to her return to work, and, although when she finished breastfeeding felt that some closeness between herself and Ellie had gone, the experience of parenthood had brought her closer to Eric.

Shirley

Shirley was 35 years old and lived with Mike, a self-employed antiques dealer, who was going to be mainly responsible for childcare once Shirley returned to work as a press officer for a trade union.

Shirley did not like to talk about her feelings. She had decided to have a baby because she felt time had been running out, but had found the decision difficult. Her sister had had a baby the year previously, and so she thought that it would be good for cousins to be of similar ages, which is what eventually decided her on the timing of the event. She had worked out the details of the division of labour between herself and Mike.

Her ambition was eventually to have a successful political career, but she did not have any clear idea of what she would be like as a mother as she had not given the details of motherhood much thought.

The baby was born after an eight-hour planned induction. She found herself at ease with the baby but very tired, and, although Mike would take over baby care sometimes, she considered that she took the lion's share of the work. Shirley was planning to return to work full-time and had arranged a nanny share. She felt she did not want any more children because: 'I'm not prepared to make the sacrifices you need to make if you have more than one.'

Meg

Meg, 33 years of age, had trained and worked as a maths teacher until she had her first child. Brian her husband was a bank manager and they had three children between them. She had become pregnant by accident and was shocked because she 'didn't want to go through it all again. I'd spent eight years being a mum and wanted to do something else.' She had just returned to teaching.

She had felt very tired throughout the pregnancy and, in fact, had become seriously ill following the delivery of William.

She had recovered though by the time William was six months and had considered getting a supply teaching post. She sometimes felt quite depressed and coped with it by trying to get some rest. She had joined the parent–teacher association at her older children's school: 'so I could get out of the house and meet new people' and was also considering doing an Open University course.

Adrienne

Adrienne, married to Philip for eight years, was thirty. She worked as a freelance cook (doing dinner parties and lunches in people's homes) and Philip was a barrister. She came from a rich family and her unearned income enabled Philip to leave his previous job and study for the bar. They lived in a large detached house in a private road near a royal park and all their health care and proposed education was to be private.

The couple already had a young son, Bobby, for whom she employed a nanny and she had another nanny and maternity nurse arranged for when the second child was born. Her second child was another boy and, because she had particularly wanted to have a girl, she was already planning a third child.

She thought that having two children was very difficult, and she especially had problems with the nanny and maternity nurse being 'too demanding'. She was a friend of Sylvia's, but was dismissive of her, describing her and her husband as 'Guardian readers'. Adrienne was particularly scathing about Sylvia's husband because he bathed the baby. She did not like to see men so involved in childcare.

Adrienne had had problems with her first delivery and had been ill for some months afterwards. However, she was clear that no one needs to be depressed.

Sylvia

Sylvia, an antiques dealer, was 29. She was married to Mark, a solicitor, who had been a close friend for some time before they started seeing each other as a couple.

They decided to have a baby because several of their friends were doing so and it therefore seemed to be the right time.

Sylvia, who had an old back injury, had an unpleasant experience of delivery because no one on duty at the time would pay attention to her pleas to choose her own birth position, even though she had been assured that her case was well documented in the medical notes.

She gave birth to a daughter, Felicity, for whom she employed a maternity nurse. However, the nurse more of a problem than she found coping with things herself and eventually dismissed her.

She did become stressed and 'fraught' at times over the first six months, and found her husband less supportive than she thought he would be. However, overall she considered that motherhood suited her, but she did want to return to work and keep something of herself intact.

Sharon

Sharon was 30 and had been married to Barry for 7 years. They had delayed having children because they enjoyed their social life too much, but in the end they felt they had to 'take the plunge'. Sharon came from a rich farming family originally and had worked as a secretary after leaving school. Barry was a businessman who earned a large salary, but, during the time I was interviewing Sharon, his company was taken over and his job was at risk.

She wanted to see herself as 'unconventional', and was determined to avoid talking about nappies and babies as she saw many of her friends doing. She desperately wanted and had a boy. She became very attached to him and felt content being at home, certainly over the first two months. However, her husband kept trying to persuade her to leave the baby with a babysitter and continue their social life, which she was not particularly happy about. So that Barry 'doesn't get bored in the evening, we have friends in for drinks, but it is still difficult to put off going out.'

She found herself getting very cross and frustrated with Barry in ways that had never been the case before, although by the time the baby was six months old she found herself getting back to normal. However, 'I think I vary enormously. I swing backwards and forwards. One minute I'm really optimistic and the other I'm down about things.'

When she received a letter from the 'temp' agency she used to work for, asking whether she was available for work, she felt it gave her a 'buzz' that she had been useful in the world out there. However, she intended to have another baby as soon as she could and did not want to work when the children were young, so she refused.

Penelope

Penelope was 41, the oldest first-time mother in the study. She was living 'part-time' with Roger who had only half-left his wife and two teenage children. She was a college lecturer and he was a local government officer. He had mixed feelings about being a father again, but Penelope had been clear that she had wanted the pregnancy to continue as it might be her only chance to have a baby, as she had believed herself infertile.

She had a difficult pregnancy and delivery which she had to cope with on her own, because Roger was on a camping holiday with his older children and could not be contacted.

Both she and Leah, her baby, were in hospital for several weeks. When Roger did arrive back from holiday, he was totally unsupportive and very stressed and anxious. He started to drink, get angry about being woken in the night and, in fact, left her several times for long periods. In the end he returned and decided to live full-time with Penelope. Although she accepted this, she felt that he had been so dreadful that she would never fully be able to forgive him. The whole experience of early motherhood 'had just overwhelmed me and I felt I was totally submerged by it.' However, she thinks the experience has overall made her stronger and that she could cope with anything in the future.

Sarah

Sarah, aged 32, had been married to Norman for six years, and they lived in a west London suburb. They were both social workers, and Norman was in a senior management post. Sarah was an ex-flatmate of Felicity's. Both Sarah and Norman come from middle-class families in the Home Counties.

The couple had been thinking for several years about having a baby, but before she reached 30 they did not feel any urgency. She had a part-time post lined up for after her maternity leave, and, although she did feel ambivalent about returning after the birth, she was relieved when she did. Her own mother had devoted her whole life to childcare and mothering and she did not want that for herself, although she did want to be a good mother. Becoming a mother has changed her: 'It's made me feel much more adult', and she believes she worries less about trivia. She did feel that she was always having to take care not to get too stressed and exhausted as that would make her depressed.

Natasha

Natasha lived in Croydon with Josh, her fiancé. She gave up her job as a payroll supervisor when she found she was pregnant, but was a trained hairdresser and intended to work intermittently working in people's homes on a self-employed basis. Natasha was diabetic and so was booked into the large teaching hospital rather than the local one like the others from her antenatal group. She had an unhappy childhood, which I agreed not to write about in any detail, and was not in regular contact with her family, although Josh had several local relatives. She herself had local friends.

She had not been very pleased to be pregnant because she was unhappy to be so fat, as her appearance was very important to her. She wore jeans or a tracksuit at home, but made the point that she would never wear such clothes outside the home and never when she was with Josh. She liked to be organised around the house and had come to terms with the fact that Josh would do very little. This proved to be the case with childcare as well as housework. She considered that she was constantly stuck with the baby without support, and, although she would not have been without her, she wanted to have a chance to have a break. 'I'm not depressed – I'm just pissed off.'

Angela

Angela, 32, had been married to Mark, a long-distance, overnight lorry driver, for five years and they already had a son, Jeremy, whom she described as a 'handful'. They lived in a small, three-bedroom terraced house. She had previously been in the police as a member of the vice squad, which she had found exciting and compelling, and, although she had left that work sometime previously, it still formed an important part of her identity. It had been her way of life rather than a job.

She had been what she had described as her 'daddy's girl', which influenced the way she thought about her social and familial role, and appreciated the fact that Mark worked at night and was able to take on a reasonable share of the childcare and domestic tasks.

She found her first son difficult to handle and also really suffered emotionally because she had become overweight. They were also financially pressed.

She always attributed any feelings of depression to specific worries such as money, while Mark told her that she 'became depressed at the drop of a hat'. She worried about the children and also about the fact that she had lost control during the birth of her first child. This made her anxious about the second birth, of her son Carey, which in the event she handled well and felt, overall, better organised. However, she did become anxious and overwhelmed with depressed feelings on several occasions, although she could only admit them to herself at the last inter-view, looking back. She found it very helpful to have the chance to talk to me about her feelings.

She found routine to be a problem and worried about her loss of independence, which she dated to not having a job rather than motherhood. She became particularly distressed when she found herself not getting interviewed for work that she would have considered beneath her previously.

Hilary

Hilary, 34, with an 18-month-old daughter was married to Ken, a lecturer. They had known each other for many years but only been married for four. Hilary was a senior local government officer, and planned maternity leave as she had done with the first baby.

She felt she had bullied Ken into starting a family because he could never be decisive, but he was pleased once the baby arrived. She had been depressed and anxious the first time, feeling things were a bit out of her control. However, she felt more confident about child-care the second time. She felt acutely that the world of the 'mother' was different from the world of work and that mothers were treated as second class, rather stupid citizens and she resented this.

The delivery was terrible in that, because she desperately wanted to avoid a Caesarean which she had had the first time, her body was badly ripped, and the problems she had while she was healing did not ease her state of mind. However, she was proud that she had managed a normal delivery.

She did get stressed and anxious with the two young children, and, although Ken clearly helped, she was not getting the degree of support she felt she needed.

Jerri

Jerri, 29 years old and expecting her first baby, was living with her fiancé, Tom, in south London. He was a self-employed plumber and Jerri did the accounts.

She had never felt maternal in any way, although always expected she would have children. Her labour had been traumatic for her in that she had to have an emergency Caesarean and, because they were not married, a midwife created a fuss to try and prevent Tom's presence at the delivery. This was very stressful. It was also a very painful delivery and she had nightmares and flashbacks about it.

She worried about the baby's health although, in fact, there were no problems. Three months after the birth Jerri started to believe that things were going well and by six months she and Tom had begun to think about having a second child and moving to the country. She felt that, despite a few ups and downs, most of the changes in her life brought about by motherhood were positive. Motherhood had made her into a more caring person who was not so much into 'image' as she had been beforehand.

Ruth

Ruth, 31, chose to leave her job as a health-visitor tutor when she became pregnant, although she eventually returned to work nearer home as a part-time health visitor. She had been married to Roy, a scientist, for two years although they had lived together previously.

Ruth's mother had killed herself, apparently as a consequence of postnatal depression, and this was at the forefront of her mind during her pregnancy and the early days of motherhood. She herself had been depressed and had threatened to overdose when she was in her late teens.

She had arranged to have the baby in hospital but, because of the 'domino' system, she was discharged almost immediately and put under midwife care at home. Her stepmother was very supportive and stayed with them after the baby was born.

Ruth developed inflammation of her breasts shortly after her daughter's birth and did suffer some embarrassing panic attacks on the first few occasions she had to go out alone (e.g. in a supermarket when she realised she had forgotten her cheque book). Overall, she felt she survived the experience without any episodes of severe depression, although she did worry about childcare a great deal.

Melanie

Melanie, a high-ranking civil servant, was 35 when she had her baby, and had been living with John, a long-distance lorry driver, albeit a graduate, whom she married two years prior to the interview. They agreed in advance that John would be the prime child carer. When Charlotte was born, Melanie took maternity leave, and chose to bottle-feed so that both she and John could take equal shares in night feeds. This meant that she was protected from some of the extremes of tiredness that she might have felt otherwise. She did have fears that John would gain all of Charlotte's attention but the compensation was that she had no doubts or fears about childcare, and thus was able to concentrate on her career. She considered that she gradually became far more ambitious, during the postnatal months and her early return to work, than she felt before having a baby. She attributed this to the increased responsibility and felt positively about this change.

Despite John being at home, she considered that she had to organise the housework, shopping and cooking, although, overall, she believed John made a better primary carer than she would have done.

Norma

Norma and Eli had been together three years, and they married a few months prior to the interview because of the baby. She was a midwife and he was a hospital technician. Norma was from a large middle-class Irish family and Eli from South America. Norma had been depressed in the past as a student nurse and was worried that she would get depressed postnatally. She was also worried about becoming the kind of mother she dreaded, who had no fun, was serious and unappealing. She had also been accepted to train as a health visitor before the pregnancy, and so felt a bit upset that she would have to give that up and return to midwifery, at least for a while, because they needed money.

A home delivery was planned, but this did not happen because, after several hours in labour, Norma decided that she wanted to have the birth speeded up and was admitted to hospital. However, she felt guilty in the end that she had made that decision.

She became very possessive and anxious about her son. She and Eli had many arguments and she felt her marriage was not what she had hoped. However, six months after the birth, she felt things had become more settled between them, and she had managed to arrange childcare and return to work. However, she felt that she had changed dramatically, having become more serious and responsible than she had felt before the pregnancy.

Wendy

Wendy and Dave had been married for four years and both worked for a local authority in inner London. Wendy, however, had a more senior post, which seemed to be the source of some contention between them. Dave had a problem with alcohol and the couple had been on the verge of divorce, but decided to try and have a baby in order to put things right.

Dave did not prove to be very supportive, and Wendy found herself cooking for him and his brother shortly after leaving hospital and was bitterly resentful. However, she felt that Dave did enjoy the baby.

Wendy returned to work when Molly was three months old, and believed that she had benefited, psychologically, a great deal from becoming a mother because it gave her an added dimension to life and enabled her to decide what things in life were the most important. Dave, she believed, did not put Molly first, in the way she thought he should, but he was a good father. Wendy considered that her relationship with Dave was, on the whole, unimproved by parenthood.

Felicity

Felicity was 31 and a scientist. She was married to Rob with whom she had been living for around six years. They had decided not to have children because he had a grown-up family from his first marriage. However, as she became older, Felicity realised that she wanted at least one child of her own and Rob agreed.

She found her work stimulating but very hard and wanted to work part-time following her maternity leave, and she worried a great deal about how she would manage her work and her baby. Part of her worry was that being a scientist was 'fundamental' to the person she considered herself to be. She also found that she worked closely and effectively with men, and the prospect of being in totally female company made her anxious.

Her son Nick was born early, over the Christmas holiday, which meant both a shock and disruption to the family plans which she found disorienting. She was worried that it took her a few days to 'bond' with the baby, which she attributed to the early birth.

In the first few weeks, she found organising her life was a 'monumental' task and felt that her sense of identity had been disrupted. Gradually, as she became more used to him and attended some work-related meetings, she became bored at being at home as a full-time mother/housewife.

Useful books, addresses and websites

Useful books

There are two good *general books on depression*, which provide insight and some clues to self-help. These are:

Paul Gilbert (2000) *Overcoming Depression: A Self-help Guide Using Cognitive Behavioural Techniques*, New revised edition, London: Robinson.
Dorothy Rowe (1996) *Depression: The Way out of Your Prison*, Second edition, London: Routledge.

Specifically about *postnatal depression*:

The NCT have published a series of booklets in conjunction with Tesco which are available free of charge from NCT Maternity Sales 0141-636-0600.
Vivienne Welburn (1980) *Postnatal Depression*, Glasgow: Fontana Paperbacks.
Jeannette Milgrom, Paul R. Martin and Lisa M. Negri (1999) *Treating Postnatal Depression: A Psychological Approach for Health Care Practitioners*, Chichester: Wiley.

Paula Nicolson (1998) *Postnatal Depression: Psychology, Science and the Transition to Motherhood*, London: Routledge.

Useful addresses in the UK

Depression Alliance, PO Box 1239, Edinburgh, EH12 8YR.
National Childbirth Trust, Alexandra House, Oldham Terrace, London, W3 6NH (Tel: 0208-992-8637).

The most easily accessible and comprehensive websites

http://www.nct-online.org.uk
http://www.freeserve.babyblues.co.uk

Both of these websites have a good homepage and some useful links that give self-help information and accessible case studies.

Sheila Kitzinger, the childbirth expert, has information on her personal website about a range of issues that would interest mothers. Of particular interest here is the section on the 'Birth Crisis Network':

http://www.sheilakitzinger.com

Notes and references

Chapter 1

1 Paul Gilbert (2000) *Overcoming Depression*, London: Constable and Robinson (p. 4).
2 Alison Corob (1987) *Working with Depressed Women: A Feminist Approach*, London: Gower (p. 8).
3 Clinical depression or a depressive disorder is defined throughout this book as an enduring state where the symptoms of depression persist for several weeks and there appears to be little that the person herself or her family and friends can do to help her. A psychotic state is one in which the individual has lost touch with everyday reality to an extreme extent and suffers from hallucinations and demonstrates bizarre behaviours.
4 Depression that occurs for no *apparent* reason.
5 Janet M. Stoppard (2000) *Understanding Depression: Feminist Social Constructionist Approaches*, London: Routledge.
6 Martin Amis *The Information*, London: Flamingo (p. 10).
7 William Shakespeare *The Tragedy of Hamlet Prince of Denmark*, The Signet Classic Edition, edited by Edward Hubler, London: The New English Library (1963) (I. ii. 76–86, p. 43).
8 —— (I. ii. 133–134, p. 44).

9 Dorothy Rowe (1996) *Depression: The Way Out of Your Prison*, Second edition, London: Routledge (p. 1.)

Chapter 2

1 A. Oakley (1980) *Women Confined: Towards a Sociology of Childbirth*, London: Martin Robertson.
2 See both P. Nicolson (1988) 'The social psychology of "postnatal depression".' Unpublished PhD thesis (LSE), University of London Library; and P. Nicolson (1998) *Postnatal Depression: Psychology, Science and the Transition to Motherhood*, London: Routledge.
3 Josephine Green (1998) 'Postnatal depression or perinatal dysphoria? Findings from a longitudinal community-based study using the Edinburgh Postnatal Depression Scale', *Journal of Reproductive and Infant Psychology*, **16**(2/3) 143–156.
4 The four interviews with each woman took place in pregnancy, 1 month after the birth, 3 months after the birth and the final interviews were carried out between the 6th and 12th postnatal month. The timing depended on the respondent's situation.
5 K. Dalton (1980) *Depression after Childbirth; How to Recognise and Treat Postnatal Illness*, Oxford: Oxford University Press (p. 11).
6 V. Wellburn (1980) *Postnatal Depression*, Glasgow: Fontana Paperbacks.
7 Ann Oakley (1979) 'The baby blues', *New Society*, 5 April 1979, pp. 11–12.
8 K. Dalton (1980) *Depression after Childbirth; How to Recognise and Treat Postnatal Illness*, Oxford: Oxford University Press (p. 22).
9 Esther Rantzen (1982) 'Introduction', in C. Boyd and L. Sellars (eds) *The British Way of Birth*, London: Pan.

Chapter 3

1 A. Oakley (1980) *Women Confined: Towards a Sociology of Childbirth*, London: Martin Robertson.
2 American Psychiatric Association (1994) *Diagnostic and Statistical Manual*, Fourth Edition, Washington, DC: American Psychiatric Association.
3 S. Lyons (1998) 'A prospective study of post traumatic stress symptoms one month following childbirth in a group of 42 first time mothers', *Journal of Reproductive and Infant Psychology*, **16** (2/3) 91–106; and S. Allen (1998) 'A qualitative analysis of the process, mediating variables and impact of traumatic childbirth', *Journal of Reproductive and Infant Psychology*, **16**(2/3) 107–132.
4 From Sheila Kitzinger's personal website: *www.sheilakitzinger.com*

Chapter 4

1 Joanna Briscoe writing in the *Guardian*, Wednesday, 10 January 2001 (p. 9).
2 B. Friedan (1965) *The Feminine Mystique*, Harmondsworth: Penguin (p. 13).
3 H. Gavron (1977) *The Captive Wife*, Harmondsworth: Penguin; and A. Oakley (1976) *Housewife: High Value, Low Cost*, Harmondsworth: Penguin.
4 H. Gavron (1977) *The Captive Wife*, Harmondsworth: Penguin (p. 136).
5 A. Oakley (1976) *Housewife: High Value, Low Cost*, Harmondsworth: Penguin.
6 P. Marris (1986) *Loss and Change*, London: Routledge and Kegan Paul.
7 John Archer (1999) *The Nature of Grief: The Evolution and Psychology of Reaction to Loss*, London: Routledge.
8 C. Murray-Parkes (1971) 'Psychosocial transitions: A field for study', *Social Science and Medicine*, **5**, 101–115.

9   Kate Mosse (1997) *Becoming a Mother*, London: Virago (p. xi).
10 G. Brown and T. Harris (1978) *The Social Origins of Depression*, London: Tavistock.

Chapter 5

1   Elisabeth Badinter (1981) *The Myth of Motherhood*, London: Souvenir Press (p. 39).
2   Joanna Briscoe writing in the *Guardian* on Wednesday, 10 January 2001 (p. 9).
3   H. Beckett (1986) 'Cognitive developmental theory in the study of adolescent development', *Feminist Social Psychology: Developing Theory and Practice*, edited by S. Wilkinson, Milton Keynes: Open University Press (p. 47).
4   Most commonly these are *in vitro* fertilisation (IVF) which allows women to conceive using either their own or donor eggs which are fertilised outside the body, and artificial insemination of the egg by donor sperm (AID).
5   Caroline Whitbeck (1984) 'The maternal instinct'. The article first appeared in *The Philosophical Forum*, **6**, 2–3 in 1974–1975, but was reprinted in a collection of essays edited by Joyce Treblicot, *Mothering: Essays in Feminist Theory*, Totowa, New Jersey: Rowman and Allanhead (pp. 185–198).
6   Elisabeth Badinter (1981) *The Myth of Motherhood*, London: Souvenir Press (p. xxiii).
7   John Bowlby (1963) *Child Care and the Growth of Love*, Harmondsworth: Penguin.
8   C. Lewis (1986) *Becoming a Father*, Milton Keynes: Open University Press.
9   Matt Ridley (1994) *The Red Queen*, Harmondsworth: Penguin (p. 240).
10 N. Chodorow and S. Contratto (1982) 'The fantasy of the perfect mother' *Rethinking the Family: Some Feminist Questions*, edited by B. Thorne and M. Yalom, New York: Longman (p. 55).
11 Sarah Clement (1989) 'Babies and PhDs', The Psychology of Women Section of the *British Psychological Society Newsletter*, **1**(3), 14–16.

12 Terri Apter (1986) *Why Women Don't Have Wives: Professional Success and Motherhood*, Basingstoke: Macmillan (p. 4).

13 L. Eichenbaum and S. Orbach (1982) *Outside In ... Inside Out*, Harmondsworth: Penguin (p. 29).

14 Denise Riley (1983) *War in the Nursery: Theories of the Child and Mother*, London: Virago.

15 The *Guardian* online reference *www.guardianunlimited.co.uk/twins/story/*

16 Story reported in the *Guardian* on Tuesday, 23 January 2001, (pp. 2–3).

17 D. W. Winnicott (1971) *The Child, the Family and the Outside World*, Harmondsworth: Pelican.

Chapter 6

1 M. Watson and D. Foreman (1994) 'Diminishing the impact of puerperal neuroses: Towards an expressive psychotherapy useful in a community setting', *Perinatal Psychiatry: Use and Misuse of the Edinburgh Postnatal Depression Scale*, edited by J. Cox and J. Holden, London: Gaskell/Royal College of Psychiatrists (pp. 233–234).

2 E. H. Boath, A. J. Pryce and J. L. Cox (1998) 'Postnatal depression: The impact on the family', *Journal or Reproductive and Infant Psychology*, **16**(2/3), 199–203.

3 C. Boyd and L. Sellers (1982) *The British Way of Birth*, London: Pan (p. 197). (commisioned by the TV programme *That's Life* hosted by Esther Rantzen who claimed that she had experiences PND with the birth of her children and believed it was due to a hormone imbalance).

4 —— (p. 198).

5 —— (p. 197).

6 —— (p. 198).

7 —— (p. 196).

8 P. Marris (1986) *Loss and Change*, London: Routledge and Kegan Paul (p. 133).

9 C. Lewis (1986) *Becoming a Father*, Milton Keynes: Open University Press.

Index